the complete

BREAD
MACHINE BOOK

the complete
BREAD
MACHINE BOOK

Marjie Lambert

Delicious and nourishing bread recipes to home-bake
at the touch of a switch

Grants Pass, Oregon

DEDICATION
Dedicated to my grandmothers, Genevieve Lambert and Letty Belden, who have always
believed in me. And with thanks to Lola, whose herb bread was an inspiration for so
much; to Diana at Quintet; and as always, to Terry.

A QUINTET BOOK

Published by Chartwell Books
A Division of Book Sales, Inc.
114, Northfield Avenue
Edison, New Jersey 08837

This edition produced for sale in the U.S.A., its
territories and dependencies only.

Reprinted 2002

ISBN 0-7858-1322-5

This book was designed and produced by
Quintet Publishing Limited
6 Blundell Street
London N7 9BH

Creative Director: Richard Dewing
Designer: Ian Hunt, Linda Henley
Managing Editor: Diana Steedman
Editor: Nicole Foster, Janet Swarbrick
Home Economists: Eliza Baird, Janet Brinkworth, Jenny Stacey
Photography: David Armstrong, Howard Shooter

Typeset in Great Britain by Central Southern Typesetters, Eastbourne
Manufactured in Hong Kong by Regent Publishing Services Ltd
Printed in China by Leefung-Asco Printers Ltd

The recipes contained in this book have been compiled for general use in a variety
of machines. Oster, Welbilt and Team breadmakers have been used to test the
recipes. For best results, always refer to your manufacturer's instructions regarding
the proportions of ingredients, especially flour to water. You may need to adjust
these recipes accordingly.

The publishers would like to thank Ceri Hilton-Jones of Team International who
kindly loaned Team Breadmakers for use in testing and photography. The Team
Breadmaker is available from good cookshops and appliance suppliers, and you can
contact Team International via the internet on http://www.teamuki.com.

CONTENTS

energy for cooking – especially on weekdays – homemade bread can turn a simple meal into something special. Imagine what a fresh loaf of dark pumpernickel bread will add to soup, or how Southern Feather Rolls will dress up an easy salad. And think how special breakfast would be if the toast were made from a multi-grain bread fresh from the bread machine. As great an invention as the bread machine is, it is almost matched by the bread machine timer that allows us to measure ingredients in the morning for bread that finishes baking just as we get home from work, or that wakes us up first thing with the yeasty fragrance of hot bread.

The bread machine allows you to make a variety of breads to suit your own tastes, adding fruit to a multi-grain bread, spice to a rye bread, onions to sourdough. Hate raisins? Substitute apricots in a recipe – or leave the fruit out altogether. Tired of the uniform texture of white bread? Add wheat germ, oatmeal, or bran cereal.

For those of us who enjoy making bread by hand, who like the sensuality of kneading and shaping dough, the bread machine allows us to have homemade bread on other days as well, on days when we can't set aside the time for long periods of kneading and monitoring the rising of dough.

With all that said, understand that the bread machine can be stubborn and some breads temperamental. Most are inflexible in their cycles and won't allow you to shave off a few minutes of kneading or to add more time for a low-rising dough. They will purée fruit and grind down nuts that are added at the beginning of the kneading cycle. And their baking cycles have no tolerance for doughs that are high in sugar or liquid – those can be started in the bread machine but must be baked in a conventional oven.

But even at its inflexible worst, the bread machine will knead the dough for you and put it through its first rising before letting you take over and bake your brioche or babka, rich in butter and eggs, in the oven.

You can still enjoy kneading the dough before its second rising, incorporating fruit, nuts or cheese that would have been shredded to bits in the bread machine. With oven-baked bread, you also have the choice of shaping the loaf into a round, a braid or a baguette or baking it in a loaf pan. You can paint the dough with an egg wash that will produce a shiny crust, or you can garnish the top with nuts, grains, seeds or sugar.

Watching a simple loaf of bread rise is almost magical. Who can resist peeking into the bread machine to see the dough rising, forming a perfect dome that will become golden crust and fill the room with tantalizing fragrances? As yeast turns a lump of dough into a crusty sourdough or feather-light rolls, it is easy to be intimidated, to believe that making bread is a trick that only the most experienced cooks should attempt.

In fact, a bread machine makes bread-baking one of the kitchen's easiest tasks. It frees the cook from worries about whether the yeast has been properly proofed and the dough properly kneaded. A novice can measure ingredients into the bread pan, press the Start button and several hours later, with no additional work, have a perfect loaf of hot bread. Later, after gaining confidence, he or she can experiment with braided loaves and oven-baked rolls.

In an era when most people work full-time and few of us have the time or

GETTING TO KNOW YOUR BREAD MACHINE

Like a car, a computer or any other piece of equipment, every bread machine has its idiosyncrasies. Each brand is different, and many brands make several models. Some warm the ingredients before kneading them. Some suggest you add liquid ingredients first, others dry ingredients. Some are noisier than others and will wake you long before your alarm clock – if you set the timer to bake bread overnight. Some give you more choices and settings – do you want that whole-wheat bread with a light, medium or dark crust?

To get accustomed to a new machine – and this book – start with a simple recipe, such as white, honey wheat, potato or egg bread. Watch the elasticity of the dough during kneading and see how it comes out, then consult Troubleshooting on pages 16–17 for help in adjusting the recipe.

Before you begin, read the recipe. Make sure you have time for any advance preparation such as boiling potatoes or mixing a sponge for sourdough. Assemble all the ingredients before starting. Most ingredients are best when used at room temperature, though some bread machines warm the ingredients before mixing them. Cold liquids and butter can be warmed in the microwave if necessary. Eggs can be placed in a bowl of warm water. Frozen yeast should be brought to room temperature, but yeast that has been stored in the refrigerator will warm up quickly enough. Although yeast dough may rise faster with a boost from the microwave, never put unmixed yeast in the microwave to warm it.

Be sure the paddle is properly seated in the bottom of the bread pan. Add the ingredients to the bread pan in the order suggested by your bread machine instructions. This may vary from one machine to the next. If there are no instructions, add liquids first, then dry ingredients. Yeast should be added last and should not be in direct contact with unmixed salt or wheat germ. If you are using the timer or if the bread machine warms ingredients before mixing them, dig a small well in the flour and put the yeast there so it does not come into contact with liquids before mixing. Fit the bread pan securely into the machine.

Select settings on the control panel according to the manufacturer's instructions. The more modern bread machines generally have more choices, but the basic differences between the settings are these: whole-wheat bread rises more slowly than bread made with white flour; sweet breads must be cooked at a lower setting or they will scorch; the French bread setting makes a crustier bread, but that may make it more difficult to remove from the bread pan. Experiment with the light, medium and dark settings to determine your own taste. Often, sweet breads will need the light-crust setting to avoid scorching.

If you are using the timer, do not use recipes that require eggs or other highly perishable ingredients if they will sit unmixed for more than an hour. I have not had trouble using small quantities of butter or milk that must sit out overnight. However, you may wish to substitute vegetable oil for butter. You can substitute water and powdered milk for whole milk when using the timer. Use 3 tablespoons of dry milk per 1 cup of water. Be sure to layer liquids first, then dry ingredients, with the powdered milk added after the flour so it does not mix with the water prematurely.

Check the dough while the bread machine is kneading it. Soon you will be able to recognize when more flour or liquid is needed. The dough should be smooth, slightly tacky to the touch, and slump just slightly when the paddle stops. If the dough is stiff and the paddle leaves ragged edges, add liquid one teaspoon at a time. If there's a sticky layer of dough on the bottom of the pan while most of it is being kneaded or the dough is so soft that it collapses when the paddle stops, add a tablespoon of flour or more. Be aware that some recipes call for a very soft dough; most of these will be oven-baked. Also, be aware that some cereals such as oatmeal and bran will absorb extra liquid as they bake.

Don't be shy about lifting the lid and watching the kneading process. It is only when the bread is in the rising and baking stages that an open lid will interfere with temperature controls. And even then it's okay to peek as long as you do it quickly!

When the bread is done, remove it from the machine and the bread pan immediately. Although a few machines now have additional controls to prevent this, in most machines the steam released by the bread will condense in the pan, making the bread rubbery or soggy on the outside. The bread should cool for at least 30 minutes before you cut into it.

The kneading paddle should be well-seated in the bottom of the pan.

Add ingredients in the order suggested by the manufacturer.

The pan should sit securely inside the machine.

ADDITIONS

Fruit, vegetables and nuts added at the beginning of the kneading cycle will be puréed or shredded into tiny pieces. Sometimes this is the desired result, but usually it is not. If you want the raisins to remain whole and the walnuts to remain in chunks, add them 10 to 15 minutes into the kneading cycle. Most bread machines have a buzzer that sounds when it is time to add the additions. (Unfortunately, most don't allow you to cancel the buzzer when you don't need it.)

If you are using the timer to make the bread and don't have any choice but to add all the ingredients at the beginning, you need to take into account whether any juicy additions such as still-moist dried apricots, sun-dried tomatoes or roasted red peppers will release extra liquid into the dough if they are puréed. Some can add as much as one or two tablespoons of liquid. If that is the case, you will want to add an extra tablespoon or so of flour.

Some sweet breads with sugary additions may not do well if baked with a timer. Too much sugar can cause bread to scorch or become sticky. Candied fruit that is added at the beginning of the kneading cycle instead of at the fruit buzzer may be shredded and consequently release too much sugar into the dough.

USING THE TIMER

If you are using the bread machine timer so that the mixing will be delayed, the ingredients should be layered so that the yeast does not come into contact with the liquid ingredients prematurely. Consult your bread machine instructions for advice – the procedure may vary from one brand to the next, and a few models hold the yeast separate and release it at the proper time. But in general, when using a timer, the liquids should be put in the bread pan first, followed by the dry ingredients, and finally the yeast. Yeast should not come into prolonged contact with any concentration of salt, oat bran or wheat germ, which may interfere with the yeast's rising action.

Recipes using eggs, cottage cheese or other highly perishable ingredients should not be made with a timer if they will sit unmixed for more than one hour. See Baking Bread, page 8, for notes on substituting powdered milk for whole milk.

LEFT Consider the moisture content of fruit or nut additions. Roasted peppers or juicy pears will increase the liquid and sugar balance.

OVEN-BAKED BREADS

Any of the breads in this book can be baked in a conventional oven. Remove the dough from the bread machine after the first rising, punch down on a lightly floured surface, and knead lightly. Shape the dough into a loaf or rolls and place in a baking pan or on a sheet. Cover lightly and let rise in a warm place, remembering that whole-wheat and low-gluten doughs require more rising time than doughs made with white flour. Baking times and temperatures vary, but most loaves should be baked at 350°F or 375°F for 30 to 35 minutes, a little longer for the $1\frac{1}{2}$-pound loaves.

I use a $9\frac{1}{2}$-inch loaf pan for most breads. The highest-rising $1\frac{1}{2}$-pound breads made with 100 percent bread flour may need a slightly larger pan. One-pound loaves with rye or other low-gluten flours will rise higher and look more attractive in an 8-inch or $8\frac{1}{2}$-inch pan.

A cautionary note about bread pans and baking sheets: the materials, construction and finishes vary widely and will affect the baking time and temperature. Double-layered pans with an insulating air cushion protect against scorching, and are especially useful with sweet breads, but breads baked in these pans will take longer to bake. Some of the heavy, expensive pans with black surfaces will brown the bread faster. If a dark, crusty exterior is not desirable, you will need to lower the baking temperature and/or reduce the baking time. If you use a glass loaf pan, reduce the oven temperature by 25°F.

Sprinkle a little flour on a clean, smooth surface and knead gently.

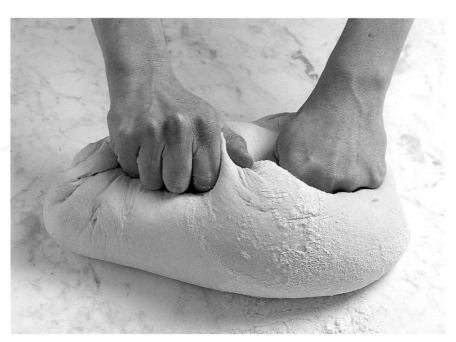

Notice the elasticity developing. The dough is neither crumbly dry nor sticky.

BREAD-BAKING INGREDIENTS

YEAST

The first yeasts known to have been used were wild yeasts unintentionally captured from the air when dough was left to sit out for hours and puffed up. That was the first sourdough, and it was baked by Egyptians about 4000 BC. Before that, bread was unleavened, made of meal ground from corn and mixed with water.

Later, bakers discovered a yeasty byproduct of beer-brewing that acted as a leavening agent in bread without leaving a sour taste. It was not until the 19th century that compressed yeast was perfected. Now, we have our choice of fresh yeast, active dry yeast and rapid-rise yeast. All the recipes in this book call for active dry yeast. The active dry yeast in little envelopes is perfectly acceptable, but I find bread rises higher and more consistently with bread machine yeast, available in 4-ounce jars. This yeast keeps longer if stored in the refrigerator. If your bread machine has a rapid-rise cycle, rapid-rise yeast can be used, but bread made with rapid-rise yeast rises less than other yeasts, and will rise very little when it is used in a whole-wheat bread.

Activated by water and fed by sugar, yeast ferments. This is why virtually all bread recipes, even for breads that are not sweet, contain a small amount of sugar. The fermentation creates tiny bubbles of carbon dioxide gas that make the dough rise. Gluten, an elastic protein in the dough, allows the dough to stretch and holds in the gas bubbles. Once the yeast reaches a certain temperature during baking, it dies and the fermentation stops. But by then, the bubbles have been captured by the gluten. The more gluten in the flour, the higher the bread will rise.

FLOUR

Many flours are available, including barley, millet, oat, corn and rice flour. Some flours have been milled for thousands of years. But only wheat and rye flours have the gluten necessary to make leavened bread. The other flours can be used in combination with wheat and rye flours, adding different tastes and textures.

WHEAT FLOURS Wheat flours are milled from the wheat berry. The berry consists of three parts: the outer hull, or bran; the small germ or embryo inside; and the endosperm, a starchy material that feeds the embryo.

White flour, including all-purpose flour and bread flour, consists of the milled endosperm with the bran and germ removed. All-purpose flour is milled to be used in a variety of ways and is made with a combination of hard and soft wheats. Bread flour, milled specifically for bread, has a higher gluten content and will absorb more liquid. It is made only from hard wheat. Because of the higher gluten content, breads made with bread flour will rise higher than breads made with all-purpose flour. The recipes in this book were tested with bread flour, but all can be made with all-purpose flour.

and not as high. It also may have a slightly bitter flavor. Most whole-wheat breads are made with a combination of whole-wheat and white flours.

Graham flour is a coarsely ground whole-wheat flour milled from soft winter wheat. It has less gluten than regular whole-wheat flour. It adds texture and a slightly chewier character to bread. The quality of graham flour varies widely. Some manufacturers have begun labeling ordinary whole-wheat flour as graham flour; others package inferior flour with wheat bran and label it graham flour. Your best bet is to buy graham flour from a reputable health-food store or mail-order baking supply catalog (see listing on page 128).

Semolina flour is a high-gluten white flour milled from durum or hard winter wheat, with only the bran layer removed. Although its main use is in pasta, it makes a delicious bread when used in combination with other flours

and adds crustiness, particularly in oven-baked breads.

Wheat gluten or vital wheat gluten flour is a high-protein, hard-wheat flour from which most of the starch has been removed. Added to bread made with gluten-free or low-gluten flours, such as rye, it will give dough more elasticity and make bread rise higher. Add one tablespoon of gluten flour for every cup of low-gluten flour. Gluten flour is available in health-food and specialty stores or through mail order companies.

RYE FLOURS Rye is a hardy grain that grows well in cold, wet climates where wheat does not, which explains why rye flour is so common in Scandinavian and Russian breads. Although it contains gluten, it does not have as much as wheat flours. Breads made with only rye flour are heavy and compact. Most rye breads are made with a combination of rye and wheat flours.

Medium or light rye flour, the most common rye flour available, is milled only from the endosperm. Dark rye and pumpernickel, which are difficult to find except through baking supply mail-order catalogs, are milled from the bran, germ and endosperm of the rye berry. They are darker, coarser flours that add texture and flavor to bread.

OTHER FLOURS Non-wheat flours are low in gluten or are gluten free. They should be used in combination with wheat or rye flours unless you require gluten-free breads for health reasons.

Amaranth flour, a staple of the Aztec people, has a nutty, slightly spicy flavor. It is high in protein but very low in gluten.

Barley flour, milled from a grain that dates back to the Stone Age, has a slightly sweet taste, a soft texture and a low gluten content. Used in quantity, it makes bread sticky; some people recommend using it in combination with millet flour, which seems to counteract the stickiness.

Buckwheat flour, made from the seeds of a cereal grass, adds a pungent, earthy flavor to bread. It is a high-fat flour, low in gluten.

Corn flour, milled from the whole kernel of corn, adds a sweet flavor to bread. It has no gluten. Corn starch and British cornflour are milled only from the endosperm.

Millet, a staple food in parts of Africa and Asia, adds a pleasantly gritty texture to bread. It is low in gluten.

Oat flour, made from oats that have been ground into powder, is very low in gluten but high in protein.

Potato flour, milled from the whole potato, is gluten-free. In bread-making, it is usually used in small quantities to lighten heavy loaves.

Quinoa flour, an ancient pearly grain flour from Peru, gives bread a nutty flavor. It is high in protein and has the health benefit of being gluten-free.

Rice flour, the flour most commonly used in gluten-free breads, is milled

The higher the level of gluten in the flour you choose, the better the loaf texture.

from white or brown rice. It makes bread with a sweet flavor and chewy texture. Rice flour made from white rice has the husk, germ and bran removed; brown rice flour includes the bran.

Soybean flour gives bread a moist texture, is very high in protein and gluten-free. It adds a slight bitter flavor.

GRAINS

Grains can add flavor, texture and protein to bread. Typically they are added in small quantities, 2 to 4 tablespoons for a 1-pound loaf. They do not contribute to rising and are not a substitute for flour. Some grains, particularly those eaten as cereals such as oat bran and wheat germ, can be found in well-stocked grocery stores. Most are available in health-food and specialty stores.

WHEAT Many forms of wheat are available as grains. The wheat berry is the whole grain and is much too hard to eat as is. It can be softened by sprouting

– the berry is soaked in water that is changed at least twice a day for several days – or by boiling with lots of water for at least one hour.

Cracked wheat is the wheat berry that has been broken into pieces. It is still too hard to eat without prior cooking, but it can be softened by boiling for 30 to 40 minutes.

Bulgur is a wheat berry that has been steamed and cracked. It adds crunch to bread. It can be added as is to bread in small quantities, or boiled for 6 minutes and drained.

Wheat bran, the outer hull of the grain, is also known as miller's bran or unprocessed bran flakes. It interferes with the elasticity of gluten and should be used in small quantities.

Wheat germ is the embryo of the wheat berry. It is high in nutrients, has a nutty flavor and is high in oils that can turn rancid if it is not kept refrigerated. Wheat germ can be bought already toasted, which enhances its nutty flavor.

Bran cereals, such as bran flakes or All-Bran, are made with wheat bran and other ingredients, including sugar and salt, and may be toasted. They add good flavor and texture to bread.

OTHER GRAINS Cornmeal, milled from corn, adds a sweet flavor and, if uncooked, a crumbly texture. It can interfere with the gluten, so use it in small quantities, or cook or soften it in boiling water before adding to dough.

Millet, widely used as birdseed, adds crunch to bread when it is added in its whole, unhulled state.

Oatmeal, the most nutritious of the cereal grasses, means old-fashioned rolled oats in this cookbook. The husk is removed and the grain is sliced, steamed and rolled. The dried oats may have trouble absorbing thicker liquids such as applesauce or buttermilk, so may be soaked briefly in boiling water before being added to other ingredients.

Oat bran is the hull of the oat and is high in soluble fiber. Oat bran can interfere with the gluten in bread dough and should be used in small quantities.

Rye berries, much like wheat berries, are the whole grain and must be boiled for an hour or so to make them soft enough to eat.

Cereals, seeds and cracked wheat give mellow flavors to wholesome breads.

SALT

Salt is critical in bread. In addition to enhancing the flavor, it strengthens the gluten. Salt-free bread may rise nicely, but it will collapse. However, salt in high concentrations will inhibit the yeast's rising action. Salt and yeast should be added so that they do not come in contact with each other before the dough is mixed. Because some sodium is necessary for bread to rise and hold its shape, most salt substitutes cannot be used.

SWEETENERS

Yeast ferments best when it feeds on sugar in some form. Sugar also acts as a preservative. It caramelizes during

baking and contributes to the golden color of the crust. But too much sugar will interfere with the yeast's rising action and cause the bread to collapse. Most yeast breads are not very sweet. Dessert breads get their sweetness from a glaze, dry sugar topping, or another addition made after baking.

Sugar scorches easily. Many machines have a setting for sweet breads and bake them at a lower temperature or for shorter times. If your bread machine does not have a sweet-bread setting, chose the light-crust option.

The addition of candied fruits is a particular problem with bread machines. When candied fruit is used, it is usually in breads that already have several tablespoons of sweetener. The kneading shreds the candied fruit and releases more sugar into the dough. Candied fruit should be added late in the kneading cycle, or kneaded in by hand after the first rising if the bread is to be baked in the oven.

Sugar and brown sugar can always be substituted for each other. Confectioner's sugar contains cornstarch and should not be used as a substitute. In small quantities – 1 or 2 tablespoons – sugar, honey, and molasses can be substituted for each other in equal amounts. Tablespoon for tablespoon, most honeys are slightly sweeter than sugar. When the recipe calls for more than two tablespoons of sweetener, substitute two parts honey for three parts sugar; e.g., 2 tablespoons of honey for 3 tablespoons of sugar. Molasses is not as sweet as sugar. When substituting more than two tablespoons, use 4 tablespoons of molasses for 3 tablespoons of sugar. Maple syrup can be substituted in equal amounts for sugar.

Liquid sweeteners, including honey, molasses and maple syrup, should be counted toward the total liquid contents of the ingredients. A change of one tablespoon probably won't make a difference, but larger substitutions of a liquid sweetener for sugar or vice versa will. Watch the dough as it kneads, and adjust liquid or flour as needed.

Sweeteners act to stimulate the yeast, and contribute to the golden crust.

LIQUID

The variety of liquids used in bread-baking is nearly infinite. Most common are water, milk, buttermilk, and eggs, but beer, wine, orange juice, and the water that potatoes are boiled in are not unusual additions. Sour cream, yogurt, cottage cheese, ricotta cheese, mashed potatoes, applesauce, pumpkin and other puréed fruits and vegetables also contribute liquid; often half their volume is liquid.

A bread made with water as its only liquid ingredient will have a crisper crust. Milk gives it a softer crust and more golden color. You can substitute equal amounts of whole, skimmed and non-fat milk for each other. Powdered milk is very helpful in bread-baking, particularly when the bread is being baked on a timer and the ingredients will be sitting at room temperature for hours. Use 3 tablespoons of powdered milk per cup of liquid, and layer so it does not come in contact with liquids before it is mixed. Powdered milk is also used when the recipe calls for another liquid, such as eggs or mashed potatoes, but you still want a golden color or softer crust.

Large size eggs are recommended for all the recipes.

Buttermilk gives bread a tender crumb and a hint of tangy flavor. It also adds acidity to the dough that is usually neutralized with a pinch of baking soda.

EGGS

Eggs give bread a softer crust and richer flavor and contribute to the leavening. Recipes were tested for this cookbook with large eggs, which equal ¼ cup of liquid. You can also use pasteurized egg substitutes. Breads containing eggs should not be made with a timer if the ingredients sit for more than an hour before being kneaded.

FATS

Fats are used sparingly in most breads but are important in small quantities because they act as preservatives and add a tender texture. A true French bread uses no fat and goes stale in less than 24 hours. Butter, margarine, vegetable oil, shortening, and lard can be used interchangeably. In small

other liquid in the dough will have to be adjusted.

Lard gives bread a slightly flakier texture and crustier finish. I don't like to use margarine because it can contain

water. If you're watching cholesterol and want a substitute for butter, use vegetable oil. You can substitute olive oil, but in quantities less than three tablespoons (in a 1-pound loaf), you are not likely to notice a difference in taste. Specialty oils such as walnut or sesame oil are strongly flavored and should be used sparingly.

If you want to cut every bit of fat out of your bread, you can substitute applesauce or puréed prunes. Puréed fruit contains some liquid, so the amount of other liquids in the bread may have to be adjusted.

Butter should always be brought to room temperature before the dough is kneaded, because soft butter mixes more readily. This is especially critical in high-fat breads such as brioche.

A note about greasing baking pans or sheets: use butter, solid vegetable shortening, or a spray. Oil will soak into the dough, and margarines may scorch.

BELOW Sit back and enjoy the rewards: great bread baked fresh every day.

TOO MUCH OR TOO LITTLE LIQUID

The most frequent cause of trouble with bread made in a bread machine is too much or too little liquid. Keep in mind that flour absorbs moisture from the air. That's why a loaf of bread may turn out perfect one time and awful the next. In humid weather, the flour may have already absorbed an extra 1 or 2 tablespoons of moisture. If you add the usual amount of liquid, it may mushroom and collapse, or develop a coarse, holey texture. Likewise, if the climate is very dry, the flour may need a little extra moisture, or it will have a dense, heavy texture or a gnarled top.

Check the dough about 10 minutes into the kneading cycle. The dough should be smooth, soft, and slightly tacky. It should settle just the slightest bit, but hold its shape when the kneading paddle stops. If the dough is very soft, settles quickly when the kneading paddle stops, and can't hold its shape, add 1 tablespoon of flour. If the dough is stiff with ragged edges and imprints of the paddle remain in the dough for more than a couple of seconds, add 1 tablespoon of liquid.

TEMPERATURE

Ingredients should be at room temperature. But "room temperature" may be too hot or too cold in particularly hot or cold weather. If the ingredients are too cold, they may not activate the yeast soon enough. If they are too warm – such as on a hot day in a kitchen that is not air-conditioned – the yeast may cause the dough to rise too much and overflow the machine.

ADDING FRUIT AND VEGETABLES

Another variable that can put too much liquid into the dough is fruit or vegetables. If fruit or vegetables are added at the beginning of the kneading cycle, they will be ground up and release more liquid than if they were added at the beeper or after the first kneading. If you're using the timer to knead the bread, have to add fruit or vegetables at the beginning, and can't check the dough during the kneading, reduce liquids by 1 to 2 teaspoons for drier additions like raisins or sun-dried tomatoes, and by 1 to 2 tablespoons for wetter additions, like shredded apple or roasted red peppers.

PROBLEMS AND ANSWERS

BREAD COLLAPSED

- *Too much liquid.* Next time reduce liquid by 2 tablespoons, then monitor the dough as it kneads and adjust liquid or flour for a firm but sticky dough.
- *You omitted the salt or used a salt substitute.* The gluten needs some salt to support it as it rises. Minimum amount is $\frac{1}{2}$ teaspoon for a 1-pound loaf, $\frac{3}{4}$ teaspoon for a $1\frac{1}{2}$-pound loaf. Most salt substitutes will not work in supporting the gluten.
- *Too much sugar.* Decrease by 1 tablespoon next time. You're getting into dangerous territory with more than $\frac{1}{4}$ cup sugar for a 1-pound loaf, 6 tablespoons for a $1\frac{1}{2}$-pound loaf, although some recipes will work with more. Don't forget that sugary additions like candied fruit increase the quantity of sugar.

BREAD HAS BURNED CRUST, BUT CENTER IS FINE

- *Too much sugar can cause the crust to burn.* Set controls for sweet bread and/or light crust. If it still burns – or your machine does not have those settings – reduce sugar (or other sweetener) by 1 tablespoon. Or remove the bread 5 minutes before the machine is done. Or bake the bread in a loaf pan in a conventional oven.

BREAD NOT BAKED IN CENTER

- *Too much liquid or not enough flour.* Next time, reduce liquid by 1 to 2 tablespoons or increase flour by 2 to 4 tablespoons (if the bread pan has room for a larger loaf); then monitor dough as it kneads, and adjust flour or liquid for a firm but sticky dough. The bread machine has little tolerance for dough that varies much from a set ratio of liquid to flour. Often, those same breads – especially sweet breads like kugelhopf or panettone – will turn out fine when baked in a conventional oven. Set the bread machine to make dough, then remove it, punch it down, and put it in a buttered loaf pan. Let it rise in a warm place for 45 minutes to 1 hour, then bake at 375°F for about 30 minutes.
- *If it is a sweet bread* and has sticky pockets, reduce the sugar or sweetener by 1 tablespoon.

BREAD HAS GNARLED TOP AND/OR HEAVY, DENSE TEXTURE

- **Not enough liquid or too much flour.** If the bread pan has room for a larger loaf, add 1 to 2 tablespoons of liquid next time; otherwise, reduce flour by 2 to 4 tablespoons. Monitor dough as it kneads and adjust liquid or flour for a firm but sticky texture. (Note: If you tap the measuring cup several times to get flour to settle, you may be cramming too much flour into the measuring cup.)
- **Too much low-gluten flour.** Breads that consist entirely of rye or, to a lesser extent, whole-wheat flour will be dense and heavy. Sometimes, this is desirable. If it is not, substitute bread flour for part of the rye or whole-wheat flour. Or add wheat gluten, an additive available at health-food stores.
- **Too many extras, such as oatmeal, wheat germ, fruit, or nuts substituted for flour.** If there is room in your pan, add 3 to 4 tablespoons bread flour and about 2 tablespoons of liquid. Otherwise, reduce the extras.

BREAD HAS MUSHROOM TOP WITH AIR UNDERNEATH, OR HAS TUNNELS OR COARSE HOLEY TEXTURE

- **Too much liquid.** Next time, reduce the amount of liquid by 1 to 2 tablespoons, then monitor the dough as it kneads and adjust the amount of liquid or flour for a firm but sticky dough.
- **Too much yeast.** Reduce yeast by ¼ teaspoon for a smaller loaf, ½ teaspoon for a larger loaf.

BREAD RISES TOO MUCH

- **Too much yeast.** Reduce the amount of yeast by ½ teaspoon next time.
- **Too much liquid, especially if there are large air pockets in bread.** Reduce liquid by 1 to 2 tablespoons next time, check kneading, and adjust flour for firm, sticky texture.

BREAD DOESN'T RISE ENOUGH

- **Not enough yeast.** Increase yeast by ½ teaspoon.
- **Yeast is not fresh.** Proof by putting 2 teaspoons of yeast in ½ cup warm water 105 to 115°F. If it does not develop a thick head of foam in 5 to 10 minutes, discard the yeast.
- **You're using rapid-rise yeast or the rapid-rise cycle.** The price for this shortcut is a loaf that doesn't rise as high. (See note on Yeast on page 10.)
- **You're using yeast that does not do well in bread machines.** Switch to yeast produced specifically for bread machines. (See note on Yeast on page 10.)
- **You used hot liquid** – over 115°F – and it killed the yeast.
- **Not enough liquid.** Increase liquid by 1 tablespoon next time.
- **Too much sugar** (honey, molasses, etc.) may be interfering with yeast. If it is a high-sugar bread (or if it has sugary additions like candied fruit), reduce sugar by 1 tablespoon, or increase yeast by ¼ teaspoon. Conversely, yeast works better when there is at least 1 teaspoon of sugar to feed it. Although some recipes, such as French Bread, get along without it, the yeast rises better with a small amount of sweetener.
- **You're using too much low gluten flour.** Increase the proportion of white flour. Or substitute bread flour for all-purpose flour.
- **Your tap water is too hard** (alkaline). Add 1 teaspoon of lemon juice or vinegar.
- **Too much salt.** This may be because you added salty extras, like salted nuts, without reducing the amount of salt.
- **You allowed the salt and yeast to come in contact with each other prior to mixing.** A high proportion of salt in direct contact with yeast can kill the yeast.
- **You opened the lid during the rising stage and allowed warm air to escape.**

BREAD DOESN'T RISE AT ALL AND IS A STICKY OR BURNT LAYERED MESS

- **You forgot to set the paddle in the pan, or it was not firmly seated and came loose.**

1

BASIC BREADS

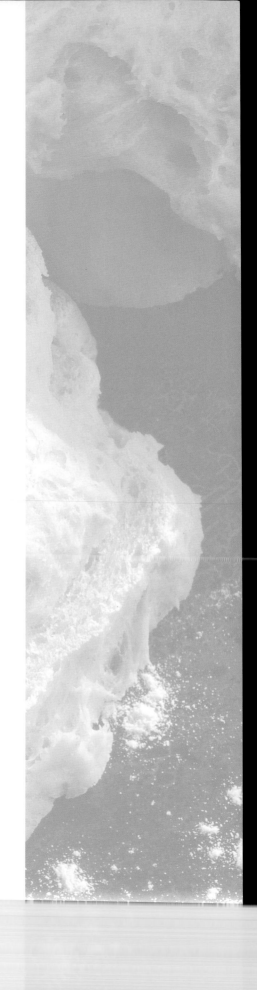

Egg Bread

*This is an all-purpose white bread, but the addition egg gives it
a subtly richer flavor and texture than basic white bread.*

1 lb LOAF	INGREDIENTS	1½ lb LOAF
1	egg	1 + 1 yolk
½ cup	milk	¾ cup
1 tbsp	butter	1½ tbsp
2 tbsp	sugar	3 tbsp
1 tsp	salt	1½ tsp
2 cups	bread flour	3 cups
1½ tsp	yeast	2¼ tsp

METHOD

Put ingredients in bread pan in order suggested by your bread machine instructions. Set for white bread, medium crust. Press Start.

Sour Cream Cornmeal Bread

*This bread is specifically for toast. Untoasted, it is dry.
Thinly sliced, it makes excellent melba toast.*

1 lb LOAF	INGREDIENTS	1½ lb LOAF
1	egg	1
2 tbsp	water	⅓ cup
½ cup	sour cream	¾ cup
2 tbsp	butter	3 tbsp
1 tbsp	sugar	1½ tbsp
½ tsp	salt	¾ tsp
¾ cup	cornmeal	⅞ cup
1½ cups	bread flour	2¼ cups
1½ tsp	yeast	2¼ tsp

METHOD

Put ingredients in bread pan in order suggested by your bread machine instructions. Set for white bread, medium crust. Press Start.

RIGHT Egg Bread

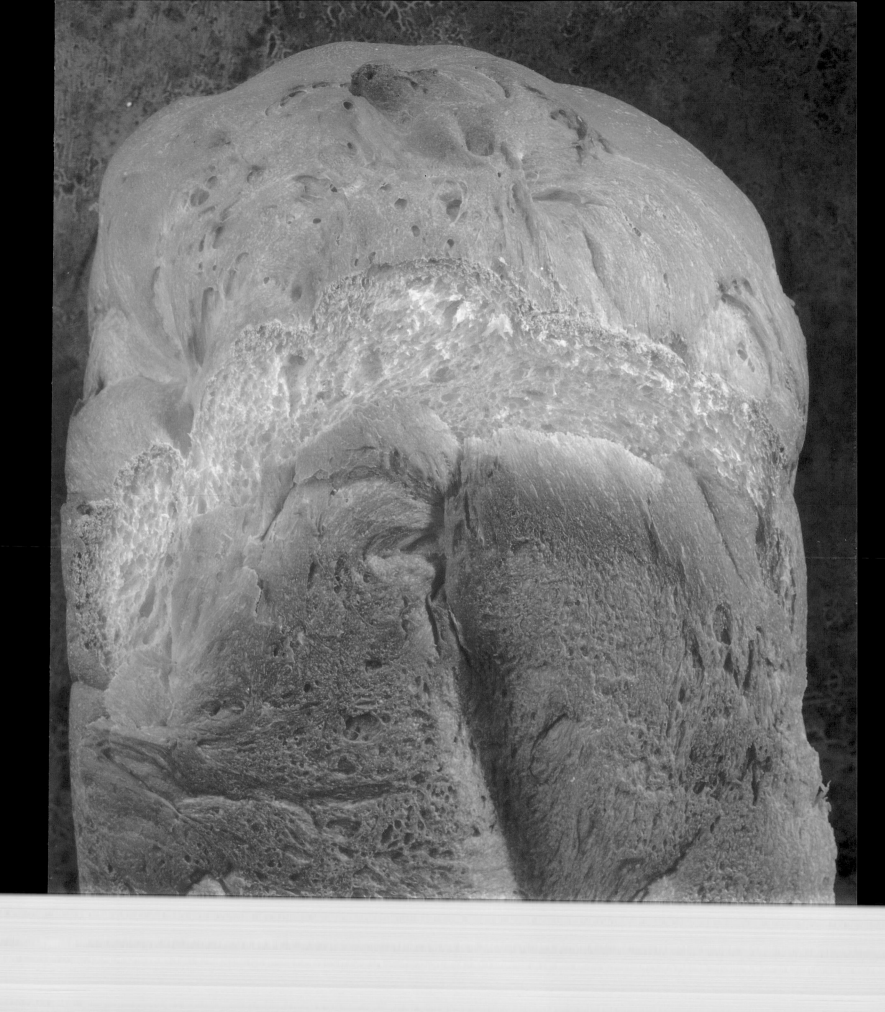

BASIC WHITE BREAD

*This is a good basic recipe with which you can try
different brands of flour and yeast, as well as experiment with
slight variations in the amounts of ingredients.*

1 lb LOAF	INGREDIENTS	1½ lb LOAF
½ cup	water	¾ cup
¼ cup	milk	6 tbsp
1 tbsp	butter	1½ tbsp
1 tbsp	sugar	1½ tbsp
1 tsp	salt	1½ tsp
2 cups	bread flour	3 cups
2 tsp	yeast	1 tbsp

METHOD

Put all ingredients in bread pan in order suggested by
your bread machine instructions. Set for white bread,
medium crust. Press Start.

HONEY WHEAT BREAD

*This is a dense, slightly sweet bread with a high proportion of
whole-wheat flour. It is good for toast or sandwiches.*

1 lb LOAF	INGREDIENTS	1½ lb LOAF
½ cup	milk	¾ cup
¼ cup	water	6 tbsp
2 tbsp	butter	3 tbsp
2 tbsp	honey	3 tbsp
1 tbsp	sugar	1½ tbsp
¾ tsp	salt	1 tsp
1½ cups	whole-wheat flour	2¼ cups
½ cup	bread flour	¾ cup
2 tsp	yeast	1 tbsp

METHOD

Put ingredients in bread pan in order suggested by your
bread machine instructions. Set for whole-wheat bread,
medium crust. Press Start.

GRAHAM BREAD

*Graham flour, a coarsely ground whole-wheat flour, gives this bread a
slightly chewy texture. Molasses subtly changes the flavor. It is good for
toast, grilled cheese sandwiches, or as a dinner bread.*

1 lb LOAF	INGREDIENTS	1½ lb LOAF	METHOD
¾ cup	water	1¼ cups	Put ingredients in bread pan in order suggested by your
1 tbsp	vegetable oil	1½ tbsp	bread machine instructions. Set for whole-wheat bread,
2 tbsp	molasses	3 tbsp	medium crust. Press Start.
½ tsp	salt	¾ tsp	

WHOLE-WHEAT BREAD

This is a basic honey and wheat bread, made with equal parts white and whole-wheat flour so it will not be too dense.

1lb LOAF	INGREDIENTS	1½lb LOAF	METHOD
½ cup	water	¾ cup	Put ingredients in bread pan in order suggested by your bread machine instructions. Set for whole-wheat bread, medium crust. Press Start.
¼ cup	milk	6 tbsp	
1 tbsp	butter	1½ tbsp	
1 tbsp	honey	1½ tbsp	
1 tsp	salt	1½ tsp	
1 cup	whole-wheat flour	1½ cups	
1 cup	bread flour	1½ cups	
1½ tsp	yeast	2¼ tsp	

JON'S POLENTAPORTER BREAD

This bread is a creation of my friend Jon Engellenner, whose hobby is making beer for drinking and cooking. He recommends eating this bread warm, with cool-weather dishes like chili, soups, and stews. Here is his description: This easy recipe produces a bold and dense brown bread with overtones of grain and nuts. The polenta provides a little crunch; the sesame seeds gives a nutlike flavor. One way to adjust its character is to substitute stout for the porter. Stout, the cabernet sauvignon of beers, sits a notch above porter on the darkness/density scale. Using stout increases the complexity, maltiness and even, just slightly, the bitterness of the bread. Beware: this variation is not for light-beer drinkers.

1lb LOAF	INGREDIENTS	1½lb LOAF	METHOD
⅞ cup	porter ale or stout	1⅓ cups	Put all ingredients except sesame seeds in bread pan in order suggested by your bread machine instructions. Set for white bread, medium crust. Press Start. After about 15 minutes or when the beeper signals time to add fruit, add sesame seeds.
1 tbsp	canola oil	1½ tbsp	
1 tsp	light brown sugar, packed	1½ tsp	
¾ tsp	salt	1¼ tsp	
2 tbsp	raw polenta	3 tbsp	
2 cups	bread flour	3 cups	
1 tsp	yeast	1½ tsp	
1 tbsp	sesame seeds	1½ tbsp	

SOUR CREAM SPICE BREAD

This bread makes delicious toast.

1lb LOAF	INGREDIENTS	1½lb LOAF
½ cup	water	¾ cup
½ cup	sour cream	¾ cup
2 tbsp	butter	3 tbsp
1 tbsp	honey	1½ tbsp
1 tsp	cinnamon	1½ tsp
1 tsp	ground ginger	1½ tsp

METHOD

Put ingredients in bread pan in order suggested by your bread machine instructions. Set for white bread, medium crust. Press Start.

PUMPERNICKEL BREAD

This is an excellent bread for sandwiches or canapés.

1 lb LOAF	INGREDIENTS	1½ lb LOAF
¾ cup	milk	1¼ cups
1 tbsp	vegetable oil	1½ tbsp
2 tbsp	molasses	3 tbsp
½ tsp	salt	¾ tsp
2 tbsp	unsweetened cocoa powder	3 tbsp
2 tsp	caraway seeds	1 tbsp
⅓ cup	bread flour	½ cup
1 cup	rye flour	1½ cups
½ cup	whole-wheat flour	¾ cup
2 tbsp	cornmeal	3 tbsp
2 tsp	yeast	1 tbsp

METHOD

Put ingredients in bread pan in order suggested by your bread machine instructions. Set for whole-wheat bread, medium crust. Press Start.

Alternatively, to make baguettes, remove dough from bread machine after first kneading and punch down. Cut dough in two equal parts. Roll each part into a thick rope, about 8 inches long for the 1-pound recipe, 10 inches for the 1½-pound recipe. Put baguettes on a baking sheet that has been sprinkled with cornmeal. Put in a warm place and cover loosely. Let rise until doubled in volume. Bake in a preheated 350°F oven about 25 minutes, or until loaves are crusty and sound hollow.

BUTTERMILK PUMPERNICKEL BREAD

This is a dense, flavorful rye bread, good for sandwiches. The dough should be checked early in the kneading stage to see if more liquid or flour is needed.

1 lb LOAF	INGREDIENTS	1½ lb LOAF
½ cup	buttermilk	¾ cup
¼ cup	water	6 tbsp
1 tbsp	vegetable oil	1½ tbsp
2 tbsp	molasses	3 tbsp
1½ tsp	caraway seeds	2¼ tsp
¼ tsp	baking soda	¼ tsp
1 tsp	salt	1½ tsp
1½ cups	bread flour	2¼ cups
¾ cup	pumpernickel flour	1¼ cups
1½ tsp	yeast	2¼ tsp

METHOD

Put ingredients in bread pan in order suggested by your bread machine instructions. Set for whole-wheat bread, medium crust. Press Start.

BLACK PUMPERNICKEL

This is a very dense, very flavorful bread, made with a coarse grind of pumpernickel flour. Although the texture is lightened somewhat by the addition of mashed potatoes, it is not a high riser. It is delicious with sweet butter alone, but is also good for sandwiches. Because the grinds of pumpernickel flours vary widely, all breads may not have the same result.

1 lb LOAF	INGREDIENTS	1½ lb LOAF
¼ cup	cornmeal	6 tbsp
¼ cup	boiling water	6 tbsp
¼ cup	very strong coffee	6 tbsp
½ cup	mashed potatoes	¾ cup
2 tbsp	powdered milk	3 tbsp
2 tbsp	vegetable oil	3 tbsp
3 tbsp	molasses	4½ tbsp
1 tbsp	unsweetened cocoa	1½ tbsp
1 tsp	salt	1½ tsp
1 tsp	caraway seeds	1½ tsp
⅔ cup	pumpernickel flour	1 cup
1⅓ cups	bread flour	2 cups
1½ tsp	yeast	2¼ tsp

METHOD

Put cornmeal in bread pan and pour boiling water over it. Stir. Let cool 15 minutes. If the coffee is hot, add it immediately after stirring in the water. Otherwise, add it with the other ingredients. Put remaining ingredients in bread pan in order suggested by your bread machine instructions. Set for whole-wheat bread, medium crust. Press Start.

HERBED COTTAGE CHEESE BREAD

This savory white bread is lightened by egg and cottage cheese. It goes well with meals and in sandwiches. You may need to adjust the amount of water slightly, depending on the water content of the cottage cheese.

1lb LOAF	INGREDIENTS	1½lb LOAF
⅔ cup	cottage cheese	1 cup
1	egg	1 + 1 yolk
3 tbsp	water	4½ tbsp
1 tbsp	butter	1½ tbsp
1 tbsp	sugar	1½ tbsp
1 tsp	salt	1½ tsp
1	clove garlic, pressed or minced	2
1 tsp	dried basil	1½ tsp
1 tsp	dried oregano	1½ tsp
¼ tsp	dried thyme	½ tsp
¼ tsp	fresh-ground black pepper	½ tsp
2 cups	bread flour	3 cups
1½ tsp	yeast	2¼ tsp

METHOD

Put ingredients in bread pan in order suggested by your bread machine instructions. Set for white bread, medium crust. Press Start. The stiffness of the dough may vary, depending on the liquid content of the cottage cheese. Watch the dough while it is kneading and add a little flour, 1 tablespoon at a time, if it is too soft. Add water, 1 teaspoon at a time, if the dough is too stiff.

POTATO BREAD

Adding mashed potatoes to bread subtly changes the texture and enriches the flavor. The recipe is based on pure mashed potatoes, with no additions. Instead of milk and water, you can substitute the water the potatoes were cooked in.

1lb LOAF	INGREDIENTS	1½lb LOAF
½ cup	mashed potatoes	¾ cup
¼ cup	milk	⅓ cup
3 tbsp	water	⅓ cup
2 tbsp	vegetable oil	3 tbsp
1 tbsp	honey	1½ tbsp
1 tsp	salt	1½ tsp
2 cups	bread flour	3 cups
1½ tsp	yeast	2¼ tsp

METHOD

Put ingredients in bread pan in order suggested by your bread machine instructions. Set for white bread, medium crust. Press Start.

RIGHT Herbed Cottage Cheese Bread

SOUR CREAM WHOLE-WHEAT BREAD WITH HERBS

This is a light, whole-wheat bread, flavored with rosemary and thyme. Fresh rosemary is preferable, but dried rosemary can be used.

1lb LOAF	INGREDIENTS	1½lb LOAF
1	egg	2
2 tbsp	water	1 tbsp
½ cup	sour cream	¾ cup
1 tbsp	butter	1½ tbsp
1 tbsp	sugar	1½ tbsp
1 tsp	fine chopped rosemary	1½ tsp
½ tsp	dried thyme	¾ tsp
1 tsp	salt	1½ tsp
⅔ cup	whole-wheat flour	1 cup
1⅓ cup	bread flour	2 cups
1½ tsp	yeast	2¼ tsp

METHOD

Put ingredients in bread pan in order suggested by your bread machine instructions. Set for whole-wheat bread, medium crust. Press Start.

DILL ONION YOGURT BREAD

*This white bread has a tender grain, the flavor of onions and dill, and a slight tang
added by the yogurt. It is a good sandwich bread.*

1lb LOAF	INGREDIENTS	1½lb LOAF
⅓ cup	water	½ cup
½ cup	plain yogurt	¾ cup
2 tbsp	butter	3 tbsp
1 tbsp	sugar	1½ tbsp
2 tsp	dried dill weed	1 tbsp
	bread flour	
	yeast	

METHOD

Put ingredients in bread pan in order suggested by your
bread machine instructions. Set for white bread,
medium crust. Press Start.

KATHY'S PEPPER CHEESE BREAD

One of my colleagues, Kathy Trumbull, asked me to help her recreate a favorite bread from years ago. It was a light wheat bread made with black pepper and Parmesan cheese, and she loved to use it for cheese sandwiches. Here it is.

1lb LOAF	INGREDIENTS	1½lb LOAF
¾ cup	water	1 cup + 2 tbsp
2 tbsp	vegetable oil	3 tbsp
1 tbsp	sugar	1½ tbsp
2 tbsp	powdered milk	3 tbsp
½ cup	grated Parmesan cheese	¾ cup
1½ tsp	fresh-ground black pepper	2¼ tsp
1 tsp	salt	1½ tsp
1⅓ cups	bread flour	2 cups
⅔ cup	whole-wheat flour	1 cup
1½ tsp	yeast	2¼ tsp

METHOD

Put ingredients in bread pan in order suggested by your bread machine instructions. Set for whole-wheat bread, medium crust. Press Start.

TIP

If you use freshly grated cheese, pack it tightly or much of the measurement will be air.

WALNUT RICOTTA WHOLE-WHEAT BREAD

Toasted walnuts flavor this bread, which should be thinly sliced, toasted, and served with cheese.

1lb LOAF	INGREDIENTS	1½lb LOAF
½ cup	coarsely chopped walnuts	¾ cup
½ cup	water	¾ cup
¾ cup	ricotta cheese	1 cup + 2 tbsp
1 tbsp	butter	1½ tbsp
2 tbsp	sugar	3 tbsp
1 tsp	salt	1½ tsp
1 cup	bread flour	1½ cups

METHOD

Spread the walnuts on a small baking sheet and place in a preheated 350°F oven for 7 to 12 minutes. Check frequently, stirring and turning. Watch carefully as they can scorch easily. When they are brown, remove and let cool. Finely chop the walnuts by hand or process in a food processor until they are the size of cracker crumbs.

Put walnuts and remaining ingredients in bread pan in

CORNMEAL YEAST BREAD

*Boiled cornmeal adds flavor to this pale yellow bread. It's good for toast,
sandwiches, or just eaten warm with sweet butter.*

1 lb LOAF	INGREDIENTS	1½ lb LOAF
1 cup	water	1½ cups
1 tsp	salt	1½ tsp
1½ tbsp	butter	2¼ tbsp
½ cup	cornmeal	¾ cup
¼ cup	milk	6 tbsp
1 tbsp	sugar	1½ tbsp
1¾ cups	bread flour	2⅔ cups
1½ tsp	yeast	2¼ tsp

METHOD

Boil water in small saucepan. Add salt and butter. Then pour cornmeal in a thin stream, stirring constantly, until mixture forms a thick paste. Cook one minute longer, stirring all the while. Remove mixture from heat and set aside to cool.

When cornmeal paste has cooled, put it in the bread pan along with the other ingredients in the order suggested by your bread machine instructions. Set for white bread, medium crust. Press Start.

BUTTERMILK OATMEAL BREAD

*Oatmeal, wheat germ, and buttermilk give this bread a soft, loose texture
and delicate flavor. It is delicious with cheese.*

1 lb LOAF	INGREDIENTS	1½ lb LOAF
⅓ cup	very hot water	½ cup
½ cup	rolled oats (not quick oatmeal)	¾ cup
⅝ cup	buttermilk	1 cup
1 tbsp	butter	1½ tbsp
2 tbsp	sugar	3 tbsp
1 tsp	salt	1½ tsp
½ tsp	baking soda	½ tsp
2 tbsp	wheat germ	3 tbsp
1¾ cups	bread flour	2⅔ cups
1½ tsp	yeast	2¼ tsp

METHOD

Put oats in bread pan. Pour very hot or boiling water over the oats and stir. Let sit at least 15 minutes. Put remaining ingredients in bread pan in order suggested by your bread machine instructions. Set for white bread, medium crust. Press Start.

RIGHT Cornmeal Yeast Bread

ANADAMA BREAD

Anadama bread is a New England hearth bread, made with cornmeal and molasses. For variety, substitute ⅔ cup whole-wheat flour for an equal amount of the bread flour.

1 lb LOAF	INGREDIENTS	1½ lb LOAF
¾ cup	water	1¼ cups
1 tbsp	vegetable oil	1½ tbsp
3 tbsp	molasses	4½ tbsp
1 tsp	salt	1½ tsp
¼ cup	cornmeal	6 tbsp
2 cups	bread flour	3 cups
1½ tsp	yeast	2¼ tsp

METHOD

Put ingredients in bread pan in order suggested by your bread machine instructions. Set for white bread, medium crust. Press Start.

BUTTERMILK CHIVE BREAD

*This bread has a soft texture with a subtle taste of buttermilk
and a more prominent taste of chives.*

1lb LOAF	INGREDIENTS	1½lb LOAF
⅓ cup	water	½ cup
⅓ cup	buttermilk	½ cup
1 tbsp	vegetable oil	1½ tbsp
1 tbsp	sugar	1½ tbsp
3 tbsp	chopped fresh chives	4½ tbsp
1 tsp	salt	1½ tsp
2 cups	bread flour	3 cups
1½ tsp	yeast	2¼ tsp

METHOD

Put ingredients in bread pan in order suggested by your bread machine instructions. Set for white bread, medium crust. Press Start.

2

Rye Breads

40

Rye Bread

40

Corn Rye Bread

41

Dark Rye Bread

42

Whole-wheat Rye Bread

43

Swedish Rye Bread

44

Onion Dill Rye Bread

44

Light Rye Bread

46

Double Rye Bread

46

Raisin Pecan Rye Bread

49

Dark and Fruity Rye Bread

49

Onion Rye with Semolina

50

Potato Rye with Caraway and Dill

RYE BREAD

This is a very simple rye bread, made with equal parts rye and bread flour.

1lb LOAF	INGREDIENTS	1½lb LOAF
½ cup	water	¾ cup
¼ cup	milk	6 tbsp
1 tbsp	butter	1½ tbsp
1 tbsp	honey	1½ tbsp
1 tsp	salt	1½ tsp
1 cup	rye flour	1½ cups
1 cup	bread flour	1½ cups
2 tsp	yeast	1 tbsp

METHOD

Put ingredients in bread pan in order suggested by your bread machine instructions. Set for whole-wheat bread, medium crust. Press Start.

CORN RYE BREAD

Baked in the oven as a round loaf, this makes a dense, flavorful bread that is excellent with cheese or butter or made into small sandwiches.

1lb LOAF	INGREDIENTS	1½lb LOAF
1 cup	water	1½ cups
1 tsp	salt	1½ tsp
2 tbsp	butter	3 tbsp
½ cup	cornmeal	¾ cup
¼ cup	water	6 tbsp
1 tbsp	sugar	1½ tbsp
1½ tsp	caraway seeds	2¼ tsp
1 tbsp	vital wheat gluten	1½ tbsp
1 cup	rye flour	1½ cups
1 cup	bread flour	1½ cups
2 tsp	yeast	1 tbsp

METHOD

Put first quantity of water, salt, and butter in a small saucepan and bring to a boil. Add cornmeal in a thin stream, stirring constantly. When mixture forms a paste and boils, reduce heat and allow to boil 1 minute longer. Remove from heat and let cool.

Put cooled cornmeal mixture in bread pan with remaining ingredients in order suggested by your bread machine instructions. Set for whole-wheat, dough stage. Press Start.

When dough is ready, punch it down on a lightly floured surface. Shape into a small round. This is a soft dough that will spread out if baked free-form. Using foil that is folded into a long strip, make a collar about 7 to 8 inches in diameter for the small loaf, 9 to 10 inches for the larger loaf. Put the dough round on a baking sheet that has been sprinkled with cornmeal and put the foil collar around it. Let rise until doubled in volume, about 1 hour. Bake in a preheated 375°F oven until lightly browned, about 30 to 40 minutes.

DARK RYE BREAD

This dark pumpernickel bread is full-flavored with a tender grain. It makes delicious sandwiches and holds up well against strong flavors. Regular rye flour can be substituted for the coarser pumpernickel flour, and will produce a smoother texture.

1lb LOAF	INGREDIENTS	1½lb LOAF
6 tbsp	milk	⅔ cup
6 tbsp	strong coffee	½ cup
2 tbsp	vegetable oil	3 tbsp
3 tbsp	molasses, preferably dark	¼ cup
1 tsp	salt	1½ tsp
1 tbsp	unsweetened cocoa	1½ tbsp
1 tbsp	caraway seeds	1½ tbsp
2 tbsp	cornmeal	3 tbsp
1⅓ cup	bread flour	2 cups
⅔ cup	pumpernickel flour	1 cup
2 tsp	yeast	1 tbsp

METHOD

Put ingredients in bread pan in order suggested by your bread machine instructions. Set for whole-wheat bread, medium crust. Press Start.

WHOLE-WHEAT RYE BREAD

This is a good basic bread with a mild taste. Made with three kinds of flour and extra wheat gluten, it is not as light as white bread, nor is it a dense bread.

1lb LOAF	INGREDIENTS	1½lb LOAF
¼ cup	water	6 tbsp
½ cup	milk	¾ cup
2 tbsp	butter	3 tbsp
1 tbsp	sugar	1½ tbsp
1 tsp	salt	1½ tsp
⅔ cup	bread flour	1 cup
⅔ cup	whole-wheat flour	1 cup
⅔ cup	rye flour	1 cup
1 tbsp	vital wheat gluten	1½ tbsp
2 tsp	yeast	1 tbsp

METHOD

Put ingredients in bread pan in order suggested by your bread machine instructions. Set for whole-wheat bread, medium crust. Press Start.

SWEDISH RYE BREAD

This is a light rye bread with a lot of flavor – molasses, nutmeg, and carrots, dominated by orange. It is good just buttered or for toast, but flavors may clash with some sandwich fillings. Try it with turkey and cranberry sauce.

1lb LOAF	INGREDIENTS	1½lb LOAF
¼ cup	water	6 tbsp
⅓ cup	milk	½ cup
1 tbsp	vegetable oil	1½ tbsp
2 tbsp	molasses	3 tbsp
¼ tsp	ground nutmeg	½ tsp
1 tsp	grated orange zest	1½ tsp
¼ cup	grated carrots	6 tbsp
1 tsp	salt	1½ tsp

METHOD

Put ingredients in bread pan in order suggested by your bread machine instructions. Set for whole-wheat bread, medium crust. Press Start.

ONION DILL RYE BREAD

This is a strongly flavored rye bread, good for meat sandwiches.

1 lb LOAF	INGREDIENTS	1½ lb LOAF
¾ cup	water	1 cup
1 tbsp	vegetable oil	1½ tbsp
1 tbsp	sugar	1½ tbsp
1 tsp	salt	1½ tsp
2 tsp	dried dillweed	1 tbsp
2 tsp	dehydrated minced onion	1 tbsp
2 tbsp	cornmeal	3 tbsp
1⅓ cups	bread flour	2 cups
¾ cup	rye flour	1 cup + 2 tbsp
2 tsp	yeast	1 tbsp

METHOD

Put ingredients in bread pan in order suggested by your bread machine instructions. Set for whole-wheat bread, medium crust. Press Start.

LIGHT RYE BREAD

This light rye bread, made with beer, is lighter in color and texture than most rye breads. Mildly flavored, it is good for sandwiches.

1 lb LOAF	INGREDIENTS	1½ lb LOAF
¾ cup	flat beer	1¼ cups
1 tbsp	vegetable oil	1½ tbsp
1 tbsp	honey	1½ tbsp
1 tsp	salt	1½ tsp
1 tsp	caraway seeds	1½ tsp
1¼ cups	bread flour	1⅞ cups
1 cup	rye flour	1½ cups
2 tsp	yeast	1 tbsp

METHOD

Put ingredients in bread pan in order suggested by your bread machine instructions. Set for whole-wheat bread, medium crust. Press Start.

RIGHT Onion Dill Rye Bread

DOUBLE RYE BREAD

This rye bread is made with rye berries, which must be cooked in advance, drained, and cooled. It makes a very dense, compact loaf with good rye flavor and lots of texture. It is best served warm, thinly sliced with butter.

1lb LOAF	INGREDIENTS	1½lb LOAF
2 tbsp	rye berries	3 tbsp
⅓ cup	milk	½ cup
¼ cup	water	¼ cup
1	egg	2
2 tbsp	vegetable oil	3 tbsp
1 tbsp	honey	1½ tbsp
1 tsp	salt	1½ tsp
2 tsp	caraway seeds	1 tbsp
1 cup	rye flour	1½ cups
1 cup	bread flour	1½ cups
1 tbsp	vital wheat gluten	1½ tbsp
2 tsp	yeast	1 tbsp

METHOD

Put the rye berries in a saucepan with lots of water. Bring to a boil and let boil for 1 hour, checking occasionally to be sure the water has not boiled away. Bite one of the grains. If it is hard to chew, let boil for another 10 minutes, then check again until grains are tender-chewy. Drain and let cool for at least 30 minutes.

Put cooled rye berries and remaining ingredients in bread pan in order suggested by your bread machine instructions. Set for whole-wheat bread, medium crust. Press Start.

RAISIN PECAN RYE BREAD

This is a tasty bread with a sturdy texture. It's good with butter and mild cheese, and for toast.

1lb LOAF	INGREDIENTS	1½lb LOAF
¾ cup	water	1 cup + 2 tbsp
2 tbsp	vegetable oil	3 tbsp
1 tbsp	sugar	1½ tbsp
1 tsp	salt	1½ tsp
2 tbsp	cornmeal	3 tbsp
1¼ cups	bread flour	1¾ cups + 2 tbsp
¾ cup	rye flour	1 cup + 2 tbsp
2 tsp	yeast	1 tbsp
¼ cup	raisins	6 tbsp
¼ cup	chopped pecans	6 tbsp

METHOD

Put all dough ingredients except raisins and nuts in bread pan in order suggested by your bread machine instructions. Set for whole-wheat bread, medium crust. Press Start. After about 15 minutes or when the beeper signals time to add fruit, add raisins and pecans.

When dough is ready, punch it down on a lightly floured board. Let it rest a few minutes. Then take it between your hands and roll it into a rope, about 15 inches long for the smaller recipe, 18 to 20 inches for the larger recipe. Put it on a nonstick or lightly buttered baking sheet. Bring the ends together to form a circle. Cover and let rise for 45 to 60 minutes.

With a sharp knife, make diagonal slashes about 2 inches apart in the top of the bread. Bake in a preheated 350°F oven for 35 to 55 minutes, until the top is golden brown.

RIGHT Raisin Pecan Rye Bread

DARK AND FRUITY RYE BREAD

This rye bread is tender and slightly sweet. It is made with ale, lemon zest, raisins, and candied orange peel, and sweetened with molasses.

1lb LOAF	INGREDIENTS	1½lb LOAF
⅔ cup	dark stout or ale	1 cup
2 tbsp	powdered milk	3 tbsp
2 tbsp	vegetable oil	3 tbsp
2 tbsp	molasses	3 tbsp
1 tsp	grated lemon zest	1½ tsp
1 tbsp	unsweetened cocoa	1½ tbsp
1 tsp	salt	1½ tsp
⅔ cup	rye flour	1 cup
1⅓ cups	bread flour	2 cups
2 tsp	yeast	1 tbsp
¼ cup	raisins	6 tbsp
1 tbsp	candied orange peel, minced	1½ tbsp

METHOD

Put all ingredients except raisins and candied orange peel in bread pan in order suggested by your bread machine instructions. Set for whole-wheat bread, medium crust. Press Start. After about 15 minutes or when the beeper signals time to add fruit, add raisins and orange peel.

ONION RYE WITH SEMOLINA

This makes a crusty onion-flavored baguette.

1lb LOAF	INGREDIENTS	1½lb LOAF
⅔ cup	water	1 cup
1 tbsp	sugar	1½ tbsp
1 tbsp	olive oil	1½ tbsp
2 tsp	dried onion flakes	1 tbsp
1 tsp	salt	1½ tsp
⅔ cup	bread flour	1 cup
⅔ cup	rye flour	1 cup
⅔ cup	semolina flour	1 cup
1 tbsp	vital wheat gluten	1½ tbsp
2 tsp	yeast	1 tbsp

METHOD

Put ingredients in bread pan in order suggested by your bread machine instructions. Set for whole-wheat bread, dough stage. Press Start.

When dough is ready, punch it down on a lightly floured board. Let it rest a few minutes. Then take it between your hands and roll it into a fat log, 10 to 12 inches long for the smaller loaf, 15 to 18 inches for the larger loaf. Put the bread on a baking sheet that has been sprinkled with cornmeal or in a buttered baguette

POTATO RYE WITH CARAWAY AND DILL

This is a dense, hearty bread, fragrant with dill and caraway. It can be made without the vital wheat gluten, but will not rise a lot. This bread is excellent for meat sandwiches.

1lb LOAF	INGREDIENTS	1½lb LOAF
½ cup	mashed potatoes	¾ cup
½ cup	water	⅔ cup
1 tbsp	vegetable oil	1½ tbsp
1 tbsp	sugar	1½ tbsp
1½ tsp	caraway seeds	2¼ tsp
1 tsp	dried dill weed	1½ tsp
1 tsp	salt	1½ tsp
1 cup	bread flour	1½ cups
1 cup	rye flour	1½ cups
1 tbsp	vital wheat gluten	1½ tbsp
2 tsp	yeast	1 tbsp

METHOD

Put ingredients in bread pan in order suggested by your bread machine instructions. Set for whole-wheat bread, medium crust. Press Start.

NOTE

This recipe is based on pure mashed potatoes with no additions. If milk or other liquids have been added to the potatoes, check during kneading and add a little flour if dough is too wet.

3

GRAIN BREADS

OATMEAL YOGURT BREAD

This is a sturdy bread with good texture and flavor added by the oatmeal and oat bran. If you wish, you may sprinkle a tablespoon of oatmeal over the top of the dough as it begins its second rising, but do it quickly so the bread machine is not open for long. Too much loss of heat will interfere with the rising.

1lb LOAF	INGREDIENTS	1½lb LOAF
½ cup	rolled oats	¾ cup
⅓ cup	very hot water	½ cup
¾ cup	plain yogurt	1 cup + 2 tbsp
1 tbsp	butter	1½ tbsp
2 tbsp	sugar	3 tbsp
1 tsp	salt	1½ tsp
½ tsp	baking soda	¾ tsp
¼ cup	oat bran	6 tbsp
1⅔ cups	bread flour	2½ cups
1½ tsp	yeast	2¼ tsp

METHOD

Put the oats in the bread pan. Add the hot water and stir. Let sit 15 minutes. Put remaining ingredients in bread pan in order suggested by your bread machine instructions. Set for white bread, medium crust. Press Start.

MULTI-GRAIN BREAD

This is a substantial bread, with the multi-grain cereal adding crunch to the chewy texture. It is dense, but the egg and wheat gluten help leaven it.

1lb LOAF	INGREDIENTS	1½lb LOAF
⅓ cup	water	½ cup
⅓ cup	milk	⅓ cup
1	egg	2
1 tbsp	butter	1½ tbsp
2 tbsp	sugar	3 tbsp
1 tsp	salt	1½ tsp
1⅔ cups	whole-wheat flour	2½ cups
½ cup	multi-grain cereal	¾ cup
2 tbsp	vital wheat gluten	3 tbsp
2 tsp	yeast	1 tbsp

METHOD

Put ingredients in bread pan in order suggested by your bread machine instructions. Set for whole-wheat bread, medium crust. Press Start.

The dough should be softer and wetter than usual during kneading because the cereal will absorb liquid during baking. If the bread sinks in the center during baking, it probably means the cereal did not absorb as much liquid as the seven-grain cereal used in testing this recipe. Next time reduce the amount of water by 1 tablespoon for the 1lb loaf, and by 1½ tablespoons for the 1½lb loaf.

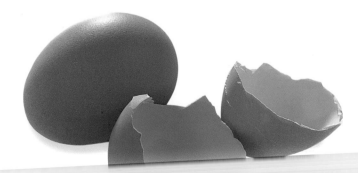

Oatmeal Whole-wheat Bread

This is a medium-light bread with a good wheat and oat flavor.

1lb LOAF	INGREDIENTS	1½lb LOAF
¼ cup	water	6 tbsp
½ cup	milk	¾ cup
2 tbsp	vegetable oil	3 tbsp
2 tbsp	honey	3 tbsp
1 tsp	salt	1½ tsp
⅓ cup	rolled oats	½ cup
3 tbsp	toasted wheat germ	4½ tbsp
¾ cup	whole-wheat flour	1 cup + 2 tbsp
1 cup	bread flour	1½ cups
2 tsp	yeast	1 tbsp

METHOD

Put ingredients in bread pan in order suggested by your bread machine instructions. Set for whole-wheat bread, medium crust. Press Start.

Oatmeal Bread with Ginger and Toasted Almonds

Toasted almonds and candied ginger give this bread an exotic flavor. It is delicious for toast or in delicately flavored sandwiches such as cucumber or cream cheese.

1lb LOAF	INGREDIENTS	1½lb LOAF
⅓ cup	slivered almonds	½ cup
⅓ cup	rolled oats	½ cup
⅓ cup	boiling water	½ cup
½ cup	milk	¾ cup
2 tbsp	butter	3 tbsp
2 tbsp	sugar	3 tbsp
1 tsp	salt	1½ tsp
2 tbsp	wheat germ	3 tbsp
1⅔ cups	bread flour	2½ cups
1½ tsp	yeast	2¼ tsp
2 tbsp	chopped candied ginger	3 tbsp

METHOD

Spread the almonds on a small baking sheet and toast in a preheated 350°F oven for 7 to 12 minutes. Watch closely and stir often until almonds are lightly browned and give off a toasty scent. Let cool. Chop in a food processor until almonds are the size of bread crumbs.

Put the oats in the bread pan. Pour boiling water over, stir, and let set for 15 minutes. When oats have cooled, add ground almonds and remaining ingredients except ginger in order suggested by your bread machine instructions. Set for white bread, medium crust. Press Start. After about 15 minutes or when the beeper signals time to add fruit, add ginger.

Whole-wheat Potato Sesame Bread

This is a hearty bread, lightened with mashed potatoes and potato flour. The toasted sesame seeds, added near the end of the kneading, give the bread its crunch and distinctive nutty flavor.

1lb LOAF	INGREDIENTS	1½lb LOAF
2 tsp	sesame seeds	1 tbsp
½ cup	mashed potatoes	¾ cup
⅔ cup	buttermilk	1 cup
1 tbsp	butter	1½ tbsp
1 tbsp	sugar	1½ tbsp
1 tsp	salt	1½ tsp
1 tbsp	potato flour	1½ tbsp
1 cup	whole-wheat flour	1½ cups
1 cup	bread flour	1½ cups
1½ tsp	yeast	2¼ tsp

METHOD

Toast the sesame seeds first, so they have time to cool before adding them to the dough. Put the seeds in a small skillet over medium heat. Watch closely, stirring frequently. As they start to toast, the oil will rise to the surface and they will clump, then begin browning. At this point, reduce heat to low, stir almost constantly and pay close attention because they can scorch quickly. When they are golden brown, remove from heat and let cool.

Put all ingredients except sesame seeds in bread pan in order suggested by your bread machine instructions. Set for whole-wheat bread, medium crust. Press Start. After about 15 minutes or when the beeper signals time to add fruit, add sesame seeds.

NOTE

This recipe is based on pure mashed potatoes with no

MULTI-GRAIN BUTTERMILK BREAD

This is a sturdy wheat bread with lots of texture and bits of flavor from the various grains in the cereal. It is good in sandwiches or for toast.

1lb LOAF	INGREDIENTS	1½lb LOAF
6 tbsp	water	½ cup + 1 tbsp
½ cup	buttermilk	¾ cup
2 tbsp	vegetable oil	3 tbsp
2 tbsp	honey	3 tbsp
½ tsp	baking soda	¾ tsp
1 tsp	salt	1½ tsp
2 tbsp	vital wheat gluten	3 tbsp
½ cup	multi-grain cereal	¾ cup
1 cup	whole-wheat flour	1½ cups
¾ cup	bread flour	1 cup + 2 tbsp
2 tsp	yeast	1 tbsp

METHOD

Put ingredients in bread pan in order suggested by your bread machine instructions. Set for whole-wheat bread, medium crust. Press Start.

WILD RICE BREAD

Flavored by lemon zest, fresh chives and almonds, this bread has lots of taste and texture.

1lb LOAF	INGREDIENTS	1½lb LOAF
¼ cup	uncooked wild rice	6 tbsp
½ cup	sour cream	¾ cup
¼ cup	water	6 tbsp
1 tbsp	butter	1½ tbsp
1 tbsp	sugar	1½ tbsp
1 tsp	grated lemon zest	1½ tsp
¼ cup	chopped fresh chives	6 tbsp
¼ cup	slivered almonds, chopped	6 tbsp
1 tsp	salt	1½ tsp
2 cups	bread flour	3 cups
1½ tsp	yeast	2¼ tsp

METHOD

To cook wild rice, put it in a pot with lots of salted water and boil for about 1 hour, adding more water if necessary, until all the grains have burst. Wild rice isn't really a rice – it's a grain, so don't expect it to absorb water like rice does. Drain and allow to cool.

Put ingredients in bread pan in order suggested by your bread machine instructions. Set for white bread, medium crust. Press Start.

RIGHT Multi-grain Buttermilk Bread

CRUNCHY BRAN BREAD

This is a chewy, dense bread with a crunch given to it by millet and sunflower seeds. Those of you who like to peek at the dough while it's kneading should not worry if the dough seems too wet. The bran cereal – All-Bran or Fiber One, not bran flakes – will soak it up. The bread is good for toast and sandwiches.

1lb LOAF	INGREDIENTS	1½lb LOAF
½ cup + 2 tbsp	milk	¾ cup
1	egg	2
2 tbsp	butter	3 tbsp
2 tbsp	honey	3 tbsp
1 tsp	salt	1½ tsp
2 tbsp	millet seed	3 tbsp
⅓ cup	bran cereal	½ cup
¾ cup	whole-wheat flour	1 cup + 2 tbsp
1 cup	bread flour	1½ cups
2 tsp	yeast	1 tbsp
2 tbsp	raw sunflower seeds	3 tbsp

METHOD

Put all ingredients except sunflower seeds in bread pan in order suggested by your bread machine instructions. Set for whole-wheat bread, medium crust. Press Start. After about 15 minutes or when the beeper signals time to add fruit, add sunflower seeds.

WHOLE-WHEAT BREAD WITH EGG AND HONEY

This is a solid bread, medium weight, with a faint taste of honey.

1lb LOAF	INGREDIENTS	1½lb LOAF
1	egg	2
½ cup	milk	⅔ cup
2 tbsp	vegetable oil	3 tbsp
2 tbsp	honey	3 tbsp
1 tsp	salt	1½ tsp
3 tbsp	toasted wheat germ	4½ tbsp

METHOD

Put ingredients in bread pan in order suggested by your bread machine instructions. Set for whole-wheat bread, medium crust. Press Start.

Cottage Cheese Graham Bread

This produces a dense, heavy bread with a nubby texture and good wheat flavor.
Use it for toast and sandwiches.

1lb LOAF	INGREDIENTS	1½lb LOAF
¼ cup	bulgur	6 tbsp
2¼ cups	water	2 cups + 6 tbsp
¾ cup	cottage cheese	1 cup + 2 tbsp
2 tbsp	butter	3 tbsp
1 tbsp	honey	2 tbsp
1 tsp	salt	1½ tsp
1 cup	bread flour	1½ cups
1 cup	graham flour	1½ cups
2 tsp	yeast	1 tbsp

METHOD

Put the bulgur in a small pan with 2 cups of the water. Bring to a boil and let boil for 6 minutes. Remove from heat and drain. Let cool 15 minutes. Blot with paper towel to absorb excess moisture.

Put the cooled bulgur, remaining water and other ingredients in bread pan in order suggested by your bread machine instructions. Set for whole-wheat bread, medium crust. Press Start. The stiffness of the dough may vary, depending on the liquid content of the cheese. Watch the dough while it is kneading and add a little flour, 1 tablespoon at a time, if it is too soft. Add water, 1 teaspoon at a time, if the dough is too stiff.

GRAPE-NUT BREAD

This whole-wheat bread is made with one of my favorite breakfast combinations, Grape Nuts cereal and yogurt. The cereal gives it a nubby texture, and the yogurt gives it a slight tang.

1lb LOAF	INGREDIENTS	1½lb LOAF
⅓ cup	water	½ cup
⅔ cup	plain yogurt	1 cup
1 tbsp	butter	1½ tbsp
1 tbsp	sugar	1½ tbsp
1 tsp	salt	1½ tsp
½ cup	Grape Nuts	¾ cup
⅔ cup	whole-wheat flour	1 cup
1 cup	bread flour	1½ cups
1½ tsp	yeast	2¼ tsp

METHOD

Put ingredients in bread pan in order suggested by your bread machine instructions. Set for whole-wheat bread, medium crust. Press Start.

HERBED WHOLE-WHEAT BREAD

A dense bread with substantial heft, this bread is leavened by wheat gluten. It will leave your kitchen fragrant with herbs.

1lb LOAF	INGREDIENTS	1½lb LOAF
⅓ cup	water	½ cup
½ cup	milk	¾ cup
2 tbsp	butter	3 tbsp
2 tbsp	sugar	3 tbsp
1 tsp	dried oregano	1½ tsp
1 tsp	dried basil	1½ tsp
1 tsp	dried onion flakes	1½ tsp
1 tsp	salt	1½ tsp
3 tbsp	wheat germ	4½ tbsp
2 tbsp	vital wheat gluten	3 tbsp
2 cups	whole-wheat flour	3 cups
2 tsp	yeast	1 tbsp

METHOD

Put ingredients in bread pan in order suggested by your bread machine instructions. Set for whole-wheat bread, medium crust. Press Start.

LOW-COUNTRY BEER BREAD WITH BROWN RICE

From the low country of the Carolinas comes this tasty, chewy bread. Brown rice gives it a hint of nutty sweetness and a substantial texture. For variety and a hint of bitterness, use stout instead of beer.

1lb LOAF	INGREDIENTS	1½lb LOAF
1	egg	1 + 1 yolk
½ cup	beer	¾ cup
1 tbsp	butter	1½ tbsp
1 tbsp	honey	1½ tbsp
1 tsp	salt	1½ tsp
½ cup	cooked brown rice	¾ cup
1 cup	bread flour	1½ cups
1 cup	whole-wheat flour	1½ cups
2 tsp	yeast	1 tbsp

METHOD

Put ingredients in bread pan in order suggested by your bread machine instructions. Set for whole-wheat bread, medium crust. Press Start.

RIGHT Herbed Whole-wheat Bread

HONEY ORANGE MULTI-GRAIN BREAD

This bread, perfect for breakfast, is dense with a soft texture, moist and flavorful. Millet and bulgur wheat add a little crunch.

1 lb LOAF	INGREDIENTS	1½ lb LOAF
⅓ cup	water	½ cup
½ cup	buttermilk	¾ cup
1 tbsp	vegetable oil	1½ tbsp
2 tbsp	honey	3 tbsp
1 tbsp	grated orange rind	1½ tbsp
1 tsp	salt	1½ tsp
1 tbsp	bulgur wheat	1½ tbsp
1 tbsp	whole hulled wheat	1½ tbsp
¼ cup	soy flour	6 tbsp
¼ cup	amaranth flour	6 tbsp
⅔ cup	whole-wheat flour	1 cup
1⅓ cups	bread flour	2 cups
2 tsp	yeast	1 tbsp

METHOD

Put ingredients in bread pan in order suggested by your bread machine instructions. Set for whole-wheat bread, medium crust. Press Start.

WHEAT GERM YOGURT BREAD

This healthy bread has a dense but soft texture. It is good for toast or sandwiches.

1 lb LOAF	INGREDIENTS	1½ lb LOAF
½ cup	plain yogurt	¾ cup
¼ cup	water	6 tbsp
1 tbsp	vegetable oil	1½ tbsp
2 tbsp	honey	3 tbsp
1 tsp	salt	1½ tsp
3 tbsp	powdered milk	4½ tbsp
¼ cup	toasted wheat germ	6 tbsp
1 cup	bread flour	1½ cups
1 cup	whole-wheat flour	1½ cups
2 tsp	yeast	1 tbsp

METHOD

Put ingredients in bread pan in order suggested by your bread machine instructions. Set for whole-wheat bread, medium crust. Press Start.

To toast wheat germ, put it in a small dry skillet over medium heat. Cook, shaking occasionally so germ doesn't scorch, until lightly browned. Let wheat germ cool before adding it to the dough.

SUNSHINE BREAD

This is a light, whole-wheat bread from California, full of dates and
sunflower seeds. It makes good toast and vegetarian-type sandwiches
of avocado or cream cheese.

1 lb LOAF	INGREDIENTS	1½ lb LOAF
½ cup	sour cream	¾ cup
¼ cup	water	6 tbsp
2 tbsp	butter	3 tbsp
2 tbsp	honey	3 tbsp
½ tsp	salt	¾ tsp
2 tbsp	oat bran	3 tbsp
½ cup	whole-wheat flour	¾ cup
1½ cups	bread flour	2¼ cups

METHOD

Put all ingredients except sunflower seeds and dates in
bread pan in order suggested by your bread machine
instructions. Set for whole-wheat bread, medium crust.
Press Start. Add seeds and dates at the beeper or after
first kneading.

APPLE BRAN BREAD

This breakfast bread, fragrant with apple and cinnamon and enriched with wheat germ and bran cereal, makes excellent toast. As the water content of apples varies, you may need to add a small amount of water or flour. However, check the dough late in the kneading stage, as the bran flakes will absorb some liquid.

1 lb LOAF	INGREDIENTS	1½ lb LOAF
⅓ cup	peeled, grated apple	½ cup
½ cup	water	¾ cup
2 tbsp	butter	3 tbsp
2 tbsp	honey	3 tbsp
3 tbsp	powdered milk	4½ tbsp
1 tsp	salt	1½ tsp
1 tsp	cinnamon	1½ tsp
½ cup	bran flakes (cereal)	¾ cup
2 tbsp	toasted wheat germ	3 tbsp
1 cup	whole-wheat flour	1½ cups
¾ cup	bread flour	1¼ cups
1½ tsp	yeast	2¼ tsp

METHOD

Put ingredients in bread pan in order suggested by your bread machine instructions. Set for whole-wheat bread, medium crust. Press Start.

To toast wheat germ, put it in a small, dry skillet. Cook over medium heat until browned. Shake and stir frequently to keep wheat germ from scorching. Let it cool before adding to bread pan.

COCONUT BANANA BRAN BREAD

This is a dense, hearty bread, only slightly sweet, but fragrant with tropical flavors. It makes excellent toast, but don't limit yourself to butter – spread it with cream cheese or peanut butter. Use a bran cereal such as All-Bran, not bran flakes.

1 lb LOAF	INGREDIENTS	1½ lb LOAF
1	egg	1
¼ cup	milk	½ cup
⅓ cup	mashed ripe banana	½ cup
2 tbsp	butter	3 tbsp
2 tbsp	honey	3 tbsp
¼ cup	flaked coconut	6 tbsp
½ tsp	salt	¾ tsp
⅓ cup	bran cereal	½ cup
1 cup	whole-wheat flour	1½ cups
1 cup	bread flour	1½ cups
1½ tsp	yeast	2¼ tsp

METHOD

Put ingredients in bread pan in order suggested by your bread machine instructions. Set for whole-wheat bread, medium crust. Press Start.

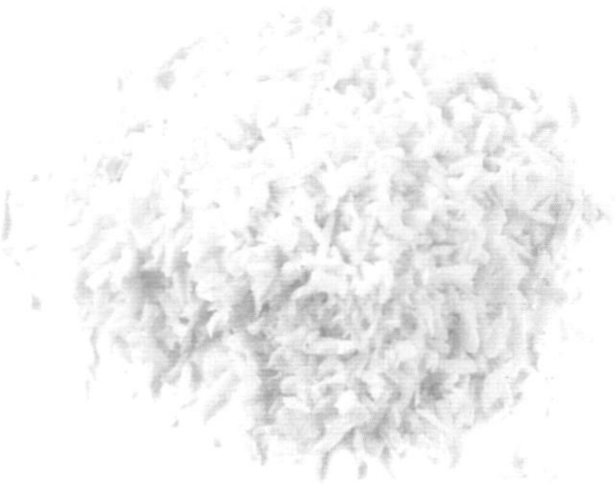

BRAN CEREAL BREAD

This is a dense but moist bread, high in fiber provided by bran cereal (not flakes) such as All-Bran. It makes good bread for toast or sandwiches.

1 lb LOAF	INGREDIENTS	1½ lb LOAF
⅞ cup	milk	1⅓ cups
1 tbsp	vegetable oil	1½ tbsp
1 tbsp	sugar	1½ tbsp
1 tsp	salt	1½ tsp
⅓ cup	bran cereal	½ cup
¾ cup	whole-wheat flour	1¼ cups
1 cup	bread flour	1½ cups
1½ tsp	yeast	2¼ tsp

METHOD

Put ingredients in bread pan in order suggested by your bread machine instructions. Set for whole-wheat bread, medium crust. Press Start.

RIGHT Coconut Banana Bran Bread

Maple-Pecan Breakfast Bread

This multi-grain bread is sweetened with maple syrup, but it is still not a sweet bread. Flavor also comes from pecans, which are added at the beginning and ground up by the kneading action. Bulgur wheat, softened slightly by boiling water, also adds texture.

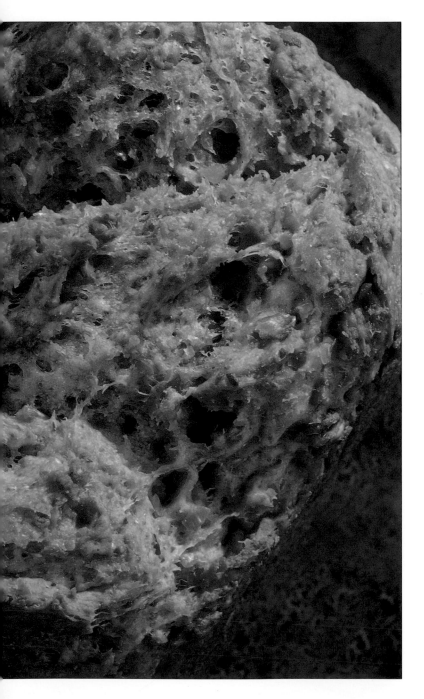

1 lb LOAF	INGREDIENTS	1½ lb LOAF
¼ cup	bulgur wheat	6 tbsp
¼ cup	boiling water	6 tbsp
½ cup	milk	¾ cup
2 tbsp	butter	3 tbsp
3 tbsp	maple syrup	4½ tbsp
1 tsp	salt	1½ tsp
¼ cup	chopped pecans	6 tbsp
¼ cup	oat bran	6 tbsp
¾ cup	whole-wheat flour	1¼ cups
1 cup	bread flour	1½ cups
1½ tsp	yeast	2¼ tsp

METHOD

Put bulgur in bread pan. Pour boiling water over it and stir. Let cool 15 minutes. Put remaining ingredients in bread pan in order suggested by your bread machine instructions. Set for whole-wheat bread, medium crust. Press Start.

PRUNE WALNUT BRAN BREAD

This is a delicious bread, made moist and slightly sweet by prunes, and fortified with bran cereal. Even prune-haters like this bread, as long as they don't know prunes are the secret ingredient. The walnuts are added at the beginning, so they are ground up more finely than usual, adding more flavor than crunch.

1 lb LOAF	INGREDIENTS	1½ lb LOAF
⅔ cup	water	1 cup
3 tbsp	powdered milk	4½ tbsp
½ cup	chopped pitted prunes	¾ cup
1 tbsp	vegetable oil	1½ tbsp
1 tbsp	molasses	1½ tbsp
1 tsp	salt	1½ tsp
¼ cup	chopped walnuts	6 tbsp
½ cup	bran flakes (cereal)	¾ cup

METHOD

Put ingredients in bread pan in order suggested by your bread machine instructions. Set for whole-wheat bread, medium crust. Press Start.

SEED BREAD

*Wheat germ, sesame seeds, and sunflower seeds add crunch
to this light whole-wheat bread.*

1 lb LOAF	INGREDIENTS	1½ lb LOAF
½ cup	buttermilk	¾ cup
⅓ cup	water	½ cup
1 tbsp	vegetable oil	1½ tbsp
1 tbsp	sugar	1½ tbsp
¼ tsp	baking soda	¼ tsp
1 tsp	salt	1½ tsp
2 tbsp	toasted wheat germ	3 tbsp
½ cup	whole-wheat flour	¾ cup
1½ cups	bread flour	2¼ cups
1½ tsp	yeast	2¼ tsp
3 tbsp	raw, shelled sunflower seeds	4½ tbsp
1 tbsp	toasted sesame seeds	1½ tbsp

METHOD

Put all ingredients except seeds in bread pan in order suggested by your bread machine instructions. Set for whole-wheat bread, medium crust. Press Start. Add seeds after first kneading or when machine beeps to add nuts.

To toast wheat germs and sesame seeds, put each in a small, ungreased skillet over medium heat. Shake the pan occasionally so seeds do not scorch. Cook until they are lightly brown. Let seeds or wheat germ cool before adding them to the dough.

MILLET BREAD

*This bread uses two forms of millet. The millet flour adds flavor, and whole
hulled millet gives it crunch. Use it for cheese on toast or for sandwiches.*

1 lb LOAF	INGREDIENTS	1½ lb LOAF
¾ cup	water	1¼ cups
1 tbsp	vegetable oil	1½ tbsp
2 tbsp	honey	3 tbsp
1 tsp	salt	1½ tsp
3 tbsp	whole hulled millet	4½ tbsp
⅓ cup	millet flour	½ cup
⅔ cup	whole-wheat flour	1 cup
1 cup	bread flour	1½ cups
2 tsp	yeast	1 tbsp

METHOD

Put ingredients in bread pan in order suggested by your bread machine instructions. Set for whole-wheat bread, medium crust. Press Start.

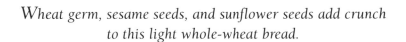

CINNAMON-ORANGE BRAN BREAD

This is a substantial bread with a tender crumb. The bran and sunflower seeds give it texture, while it gets flavor from cinnamon, orange zest, and the nuttiness of the sunflower seeds. It makes excellent toast. Use a bran cereal such as All-Bran or Fiber One, not flakes.

1lb LOAF	INGREDIENTS	1½lb LOAF
¼ cup	water	6 tbsp
½ cup	milk	¾ cup
1 tbsp	butter	1½ tbsp
2 tbsp	honey	3 tbsp
1 tsp	cinnamon	1½ tsp
1 tsp	grated orange zest	1½ tsp
1 tsp	salt	1½ tsp
⅓ cup	bran cereal	½ cup
¾ cup	whole-wheat flour	1 cup + 2 tbsp
1 cup	bread flour	1½ cups
1½ tsp	yeast	2¼ tsp
2 tbsp	raw sunflower seeds	3 tbsp

METHOD

Put all ingredients except sunflower seeds in bread pan in order suggested by your bread machine instructions. Set for whole-wheat bread, medium crust. Press Start. After about 15 minutes or when the beeper signals time to add fruit, add sunflower seeds.

CRACKED WHEAT BUTTERMILK BREAD

*This is a moist, hearty whole-wheat bread, with cracked wheat adding
texture and heft. It is a good sandwich bread.*

1 lb LOAF	INGREDIENTS	1½ lb LOAF	METHOD
¼ cup	cracked wheat	6 tbsp	Put cracked wheat in small saucepan with 1 to 2 cups water. Bring to a boil, then reduce heat to medium and let boil for 6 minutes. Remove from heat and drain thoroughly. Let wheat cool about 15 minutes.
9 tbsp	buttermilk	⅞ cup	
2 tbsp	butter	3 tbsp	
2 tbsp	honey	3 tbsp	
1 tsp	salt	1½ tsp	
¼ tsp	baking soda	¼ tsp	Put cooked wheat and all other ingredients in bread pan in order suggested by your bread machine instructions. Set for whole-wheat bread, medium crust. Press Start.
1 cup	bread flour	1½ cups	
1 cup	whole-wheat flour	1½ cups	

4

VEGETABLE BREADS

80

Carrot Ginger Whole-wheat Bread

81

Sweet Potato Whole-wheat Bread

82

Potato Bread with Roasted Garlic

84

Jalapeño Cheese Bread

85

Onion Cheese Bread

86

Basil Tomato Parmesan Bread

87

Pumpkin Graham Bread

88

Olive Cheese Bread

89

Oatmeal Walnut Bread

90

Zucchini Bread

90

Cottage Cheese Dill Bread

92

Italian Herb Bread

93

Semolina Bread with Zucchini and Millet

95

Applesauce Oat Bran Bread

95

Cuban Bread with Yuca

96

Applesauce Hazelnut Bread

96

Ricotta Walnut Herb Bread

97

Sweet Red Pepper Sage Bread

98

Date Granola Bread

98

Sweet Potato Bread

CARROT GINGER WHOLE-WHEAT BREAD

This is a bread with a light texture, mildly flavored by carrots and ginger. Despite the exotic sound, it is a fine sandwich bread that won't clash with most ingredients.

1lb LOAF	INGREDIENTS	1½lb LOAF
¼ cup	water	6 tbsp
¼ cup	milk	6 tbsp
½ cup	grated carrots, lightly packed	¾ cup
2 tbsp	vegetable oil	3 tbsp
2 tbsp	honey	3 tbsp
1 tsp	salt	1½ tsp
1½ tsp	ground ginger	2¼ tsp
3 tbsp	wheat germ	4½ tbsp
1¼ cups	bread flour	1¾ cups + 2 tbsp
¾ cup	whole-wheat flour	1 cup + 2 tbsp
1½ tsp	yeast	2¼ tsp

METHOD

Put ingredients in bread pan in order suggested by your bread machine instructions. Set for whole-wheat bread, medium crust. Press Start.

SWEET POTATO WHOLE-WHEAT BREAD

The flavor of sweet potatoes is very subtle in this bread, and it is not a sweet bread. The bulgur gives it a nice texture. It is good for sandwiches as well as toast.

1lb LOAF	INGREDIENTS	1½lb LOAF
¼ cup	bulgur	6 tbsp
2 cups	water	2 cups
3 tbsp	milk	4½ tbsp
⅔ cup	puréed, cooked sweet potato	1 cup
2 tbsp	butter	3 tbsp
2 tbsp	molasses	3 tbsp
1 tsp	salt	1½ tsp
1 cup	bread flour	1½ cups
1 cup	whole-wheat flour	1½ cups
2 tsp	yeast	1 tbsp

METHOD

Put the bulgur wheat in a small pan with the water. Bring to a boil and let boil for 6 minutes. Remove from heat and drain. Let cool 15 minutes. Blot with paper towel to absorb excess moisture.

Put bulgur and remaining ingredients in bread pan in order suggested by your bread machine instructions. Set for whole-wheat bread, medium crust. Press Start.

POTATO BREAD WITH ROASTED GARLIC

Although this bread will fill your kitchen with heady fragrances of cheese and garlic, the flavor of the bread is subtle. It is best served warm with butter.

1lb LOAF	INGREDIENTS	1½lb LOAF
6–8	garlic cloves	10–12
1 tbsp	olive oil	1 tbsp
2 tbsp	milk	3 tbsp
¼ cup	water	6 tbsp
½ cup	mashed potatoes	¾ cup
2 tbsp	butter	3 tbsp
1 tbsp	sugar	1½ tbsp
⅓ cup	grated Parmesan cheese	½ cup
½ tsp	fresh-ground black pepper	¾ tsp
1 tsp	salt	1½ tsp
2 cups	bread flour	3 cups
2 tsp	yeast	1 tbsp

METHOD

Preheat oven to 350°F. Put garlic cloves, unpeeled, in a square of aluminum foil. Brush with the olive oil. Fold the foil around the cloves. Bake for 30 minutes, or until garlic is soft. Let sit until cloves are cool enough to handle. Then cut open the top of each clove and squeeze out the garlic.

Put the garlic and other ingredients in bread pan in order suggested by your bread machine instructions. Set for white bread, medium crust. Press Start.

NOTE

This recipe is based on pure mashed potatoes with no additions. If milk or other liquids have been added to the potatoes, check during kneading and add a little flour if dough is too wet.

TIP

If you use freshly grated cheese, pack it tightly or much of the measurement will be air.

Jalapeño Cheese Bread

With one jalapeño chile, this is a pleasantly spicy bread. With two jalapeños, it's hot but not scorching. The cheese flavor is more subtle, while the cornmeal gives it a finer texture.

1lb LOAF	INGREDIENTS	1½lb LOAF
⅓ cup	cornmeal	½ cup
⅓ cup	boiling water	½ cup
½ cup	buttermilk	¾ cup
1 tbsp	butter	1½ tbsp
1 tbsp	sugar	1½ tbsp
⅔ cup	grated Cheddar cheese	1 cup
1 or 2	jalapeño chiles, chopped	2 or 3
3 tbsp	chopped fresh cilantro	4½ tbsp
1 tsp	salt	1½ tsp
2 cups	bread flour	3 cups
1½ tsp	yeast	2¼ tsp

METHOD

Put the cornmeal in the bread machine pan. Add the boiling water, stir well. Let cool at least 10 minutes. Put remaining ingredients in bread pan in order suggested by your bread machine instructions. Set for white bread, medium crust. Press Start.

TIP

If you use freshly grated cheese, pack it tightly or much of the measurement will be air.

ONION CHEESE BREAD

*The onion and cheese flavors are not as strong as you might expect in this bread,
which makes good sandwiches.*

1lb LOAF	INGREDIENTS	1½lb LOAF
2 tbsp	water	3 tbsp
½ cup	milk	¾ cup
1 tbsp	butter	1½ tbsp
1 tbsp	sugar	1½ tbsp
4	scallions, thinly sliced	6
⅔ cup	shredded Swiss cheese	1 cup

METHOD

Put ingredients in bread pan in order suggested by your
bread machine instructions. Set for white bread,
medium crust. Press Start.

BASIL TOMATO PARMESAN BREAD

This is a moist and savory bread, seasoned with basil, Parmesan cheese, and sun-dried tomatoes. Serve it with sweet butter, or use it for sandwiches. You can add the tomatoes at the beginning or after the initial kneading. If you add the tomatoes at the same time as the other ingredients, the bread will be a deep red-orange with very few bits of tomato.

1 lb LOAF	INGREDIENTS	1½ lb LOAF
½ cup	water	¾ cup
¼ cup	milk	6 tbsp
2 tbsp	olive oil	3 tbsp
1 tsp	sugar	1½ tsp
1 tsp	salt	1½ tsp
2 tsp	dried basil	3 tsp
⅓ cup	grated Parmesan cheese	½ cup
2 cups	bread flour	3 cups
2 tsp	yeast	1 tbsp
¼ cup	chopped sun-dried tomatoes	6 tbsp

METHOD

Add all ingredients except tomatoes in the order suggested by bread machine instructions. Set machine for white bread, medium crust. Press Start.

If tomatoes are oil-packed, blot them dry. (Tomato oil may be used instead of all or part of the olive oil in the recipe.) Chop tomatoes or cut with kitchen scissors. Add them to the dough after the first kneading, or when the beeper indicates it is time to add fruit.

PUMPKIN GRAHAM BREAD

Don't be put off by the orange hues of this tasty bread. It has a slightly chewy texture, a subtle pumpkin flavor and a spicy aroma. It is not a sweet bread, but is delicious for toast with jam and makes a good turkey sandwich.

1lb LOAF	INGREDIENTS	1½lb LOAF
⅓ cup	milk	½ cup
¾ cup	puréed pumpkin	1 cup + 2 tbsp
2 tbsp	butter	3 tbsp
2 tbsp	sugar	3 tbsp
1 tsp	cinnamon	1½ tsp
½ tsp	ground nutmeg	¾ tsp
1 tsp	salt	1½ tsp
1 cup	bread flour	1½ cups
1 cup	graham flour	1½ cups
1½ tsp	yeast	2¼ tsp

METHOD

Put ingredients in bread pan in order suggested by your bread machine instructions. Set for whole-wheat bread, medium crust. Press Start.

The stiffness of the dough may vary, depending on the liquid content of the pumpkin. Watch the dough while it is kneading and add a little flour, 1 tablespoon at a time, if it is too soft. Add water, 1 teaspoon at a time, if the dough is too stiff.

Olive Cheese Bread

This is an assertive bread, flavored with green olives, feta cheese, sun-dried tomatoes, and thyme. Serve it with pasta, homemade tomato soup, antipasto, or salad. It can be baked in the bread machine, or shaped into a round loaf and baked in the oven.

1 lb LOAF	INGREDIENTS	1½ lb LOAF
⅔ cup	water	1 cup
2 tbsp	olive oil	3 tbsp
1 tbsp	sugar	1½ tbsp
½ tsp	dried thyme	¾ tsp
1 tsp	salt	1½ tsp
2 cups	bread flour	3 cups
1½ tsp	yeast	2¼ tsp
⅓ cup	crumbled feta cheese	½ cup
¼ cup	coarsely chopped green olives	6 tbsp
2 tbsp	chopped sun-dried tomatoes	3 tbsp
2 tbsp	bread flour	3 tbsp

METHOD

Put first seven ingredients in bread pan in order suggested by your bread machine instructions. Set for white bread, medium crust. Press Start. Toss remaining ingredients with flour, then add them to the dough after first kneading or at the beeper.

To bake in the oven, set the bread machine for dough stage. When dough is ready, remove and punch down. Shape into a round loaf. Put on a baking sheet that has been sprinkled with cornmeal. Cover loosely and put in a warm place to rise until doubled in volume. Brush the surface with a glaze of 1 egg mixed with 1 tbsp water, and bake in a preheated 350°F oven until golden, about 25 minutes.

Oatmeal Walnut Bread

Old-fashioned rolled oats add a nice texture to this breakfast bread.

1 lb LOAF	INGREDIENTS	1½ lb LOAF
½ cup	milk	¾ cup
¼ cup	water	6 tbsp
1 tbsp	butter	1½ tbsp
2 tbsp	honey	3 tbsp
1 tsp	salt	1½ tsp
1¾ cups	bread flour	2⅔ cups
½ cup	rolled oats	¾ cup
½ cup	chopped walnuts	¾ cup
1½ tsp	yeast	2¼ tsp

METHOD

Put ingredients in bread pan in order suggested by your bread machine instructions. Set for white bread, medium crust. Press Start.

RIGHT Olive Cheese Bread

ZUCCHINI BREAD

This is a medium-weight whole-wheat bread. Cottage cheese lightens it, bulgur wheat adds crunch, and zucchini adds subtle flavor. It makes excellent toast and is also good for sandwiches. The amount of water needed may vary, depending on the water content of the cottage cheese, so check the dough during kneading.

1 lb LOAF	INGREDIENTS	1½ lb LOAF
½ cup	cottage cheese	¾ cup
¼ cup	water	6 tbsp
½ cup	grated raw zucchini	¾ cup
2 tbsp	butter	3 tbsp
1 tbsp	sugar	1½ tbsp
1 tsp	salt	1½ tsp
3 tbsp	bulgur wheat	4½ tbsp
⅔ cup	whole-wheat flour	1 cup
1⅓ cups	bread flour	2 cups
1½ tsp	yeast	2¼ tsp

METHOD

Put ingredients in bread pan in order suggested by your bread machine instructions. Set for whole wheat-bread, medium crust. Press Start.

COTTAGE CHEESE DILL BREAD

Cottage cheese gives this bread a feathery light texture. Try it in a sandwich. The amount of water needed may vary slightly, depending on the liquid content of the cottage cheese.

1 lb LOAF	INGREDIENTS	1½ lb LOAF
⅔ cup	cottage cheese	1 cup
1	egg	1 egg + 1 yolk
2½ tbsp	water	4 tbsp
1 tbsp	butter	1½ tbsp
1 tbsp	honey	1½ tbsp
½ tsp	salt	¾ tsp
1½ cups	bread flour	2¼ cups
½ cup	whole-wheat flour	¾ cup
2 tsp	dried dill	1 tbsp
1½ tsp	yeast	2¼ tsp

METHOD

Put ingredients in bread pan in order suggested by your bread machine instructions. Set for whole-wheat bread, medium crust. Press Start.

RIGHT Zucchini Bread

ITALIAN HERB BREAD

This is a delicious white bread, seasoned with garlic and Italian herbs. It makes delicious cheese or meat sandwiches, and is an excellent dinner bread.

1 lb LOAF	INGREDIENTS	1½ lb LOAF
2 tbsp	olive oil	3 tbsp
1	clove garlic, pressed	1 or 2
1 tsp	dried basil	1½ tsp
½ tsp	dried oregano	¾ tsp
¼ tsp	dried rosemary	¼ tsp
¼ tsp	dried thyme	½ tsp
½ cup	water	¾ cup
¼ cup	milk	6 tbsp
1 tsp	sugar	1½ tsp
1 tsp	salt	1½ tsp
2 cups	bread flour	3 cups
1½ tsp	yeast	2¼ tsp

METHOD

Heat oil in a small skillet. Add the garlic and herbs. Saute for 2 minutes, taking care not to let the garlic scorch or it will turn bitter. If necessary, remove the pan from the stove. The herbs will continuing cooking in the oil's heat.

Put the herb oil and remaining ingredients in bread pan in order suggested by your bread machine instructions. Set for white bread, medium crust. Press Start.

Semolina Bread with Zucchini and Millet

This is a light-textured white bread that is made slightly more crusty by the semolina flour, crunchy with millet and just a hint of zucchini. Use it for sandwiches and toast.

1lb LOAF	INGREDIENTS	1½lb LOAF
½ cup	buttermilk	¾ cup
2 tbsp	olive oil	3 tbsp
1 tbsp	sugar	1½ tbsp
½ cup	grated raw zucchini	¾ cup
½ tsp	baking soda	¾ tsp
2 tbsp	millet seed	3 tbsp
1 tsp	salt	1½ tsp

METHOD

Before starting the bread, blot the grated zucchini to absorb any excess moisture.

Put ingredients in bread pan in order suggested by your bread machine instructions. Set for white bread, medium crust. Press Start.

Check consistency of dough during kneading, adding more water if needed.

Applesauce Oat Bran Bread

This is a light bread with a delicate flavor and texture added by the oat bran and wheat germ. It makes excellent toast.

1lb LOAF	INGREDIENTS	1½lb LOAF
⅓ cup	milk	½ cup
½ cup	unsweetened applesauce	¾ cup
1 tbsp	butter	1½ tbsp
2 tbsp	honey	3 tbsp
½ tsp	cinnamon	¾ tsp
¼ tsp	ground cloves	½ tsp
1 tsp	salt	1½ tsp
1⅔ cups	bread flour	2½ cups
⅓ cup	oat bran	½ cup
2 tbsp	toasted wheat germ	3 tbsp
1½ tsp	yeast	2¼ tsp

METHOD

Put ingredients in bread pan in order suggested by your bread machine instructions. Set for white bread, medium crust. Press Start.

The amount of liquid needed may vary, depending on how watery the applesauce is, so check the dough after it has been kneading for several minutes.

LEFT Applesauce
Oat Bran Bread

Cuban Bread with Yuca

Yuca, also known as cassava, is a tuber whose potato-like flesh is widely used in the Caribbean. It is available in some ethnic markets. In this recipe, it adds density and subtle flavor. Plain mashed potatoes may be substituted for the yuca.

1lb LOAF	INGREDIENTS	1½lb LOAF
⅔ cup	mashed yuca (see tip)	1 cup
½ cup	water	⅔ cup
1 tbsp	sugar	1½ tbsp
1 tsp	salt	1½ tsp
2 cups	bread flour	3 cups
1½ tsp	yeast	2¼ tsp
	several bay leaves	

METHOD

Put all ingredients except bay leaves in bread pan in order suggested by your bread machine instructions. Set for white bread, dough stage. Press Start.

When dough is ready, punch it down on a lightly floured board. Let it rest a few minutes. Then take it between your hands and roll it into a fat log, 10 to 12 inches long for the smaller loaf, 15 to 18 inches for the larger loaf. Put it on a baking sheet that has been sprinkled with cornmeal or in a buttered baguette mold. Cover and let rise 45 to 60 minutes. With a sharp knife, make several diagonal slashes, about a half-inch deep, across the width of the loaf. Stick a bay leaf in each cut. Bake in a preheated 375°F oven until top is golden, about 30 to 40 minutes.

TIP

To cook yuca, quarter lengthwise. Remove fibrous core. Pare away dark peel and pink underlayer. Cut into chunks. Put in a large saucepan and cover with cold

APPLESAUCE HAZELNUT BREAD

This apple-flavored bread is only slightly sweet, but fragrant with spice. Oatmeal and hazelnuts give it a nice texture. It is best as a breakfast bread.

1 lb LOAF	INGREDIENTS	1½ lb LOAF
½ cup	old-fashioned rolled oats	¾ cup
⅓ cup	boiling water	½ cup
⅓ cup	unsweetened applesauce	½ cup
¼ cup	water	90 ml (3 fl oz)
1 tbsp	vegetable oil	1½ tbsp
1 tbsp	honey	1½ tbsp
½ tsp	cinnamon	¾ tsp
¼ tsp	allspice	½ tsp
2 tbsp	powdered milk	3 tbsp
½ tsp	salt	¾ tsp
1¾ cups	bread flour	2½ cups
1½ tsp	yeast	2¼ tsp
40 g (1½ oz)	chopped toasted hazelnuts	60 g (2¼ oz)

METHOD

Put oatmeal in bread pan. Pour boiling water over oatmeal. Stir and let sit 15 minutes. Add remaining ingredients, except hazelnuts, in order suggested by your bread machine instructions. Set for white bread, medium crust. Press Start. Add hazelnuts after first kneading or at beeper.

The applesauce should be thick. If it is runny, simmer it in a small saucepan to evaporate excess water. Measure the applesauce after cooking, since water may account for nearly half the volume of some store-bought applesauce. Also check the dough after five minutes of kneading and add water or flour if needed. Omit the honey if the applesauce is pre-sweetened.

RICOTTA WALNUT HERB BREAD

Try this bread with meatloaf sandwiches, pasta, light soups, and salads.

1 lb LOAF	INGREDIENTS	1½ lb LOAF
2 tbsp	olive oil	3 tbsp
1 tsp	dried basil	1½ tsp
⅔ cup	ricotta cheese	1 cup
1	egg	1 egg + 1 yolk
3 tbsp	milk	4½ tbsp
2 tsp	sugar	1 tbsp
1 tsp	salt	1½ tsp
2 cups	bread flour	3 cups
1½ tsp	yeast	2¼ tsp
¼ cup	chopped walnuts	6 tbsp

METHOD

Heat oil in a skillet. Add basil. Cook for 1 minute over low heat. Remove from heat and let it cool.

Drain off any watery liquid from the ricotta cheese.

Put cooled basil oil, drained ricotta, and all remaining ingredients except walnuts in bread pan in order suggested by your bread machine instructions. Set for white bread, medium crust. Press Start. Add the walnuts at the beeper or after the first kneading.

Sweet Red Pepper Sage Bread

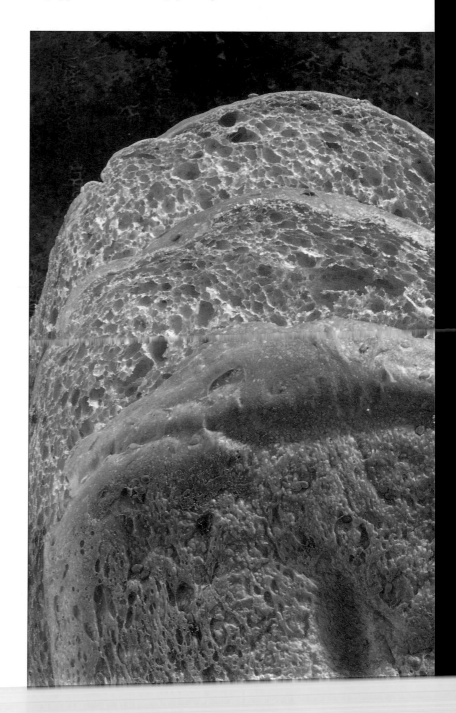

Made with semolina flour, this is a very light bread. The sage, toasted sesame seeds, and roasted sweet red bell peppers make it very flavorful.

1 lb LOAF	INGREDIENTS	1½ lb LOAF
½ cup	milk	¾ cup
⅓ cup	chopped, roasted sweet red peppers	½ cup
2 tbsp	olive oil	3 tbsp
1 tbsp	sugar	1½ tbsp
3 tbsp	toasted sesame seeds	4½ tbsp
1 tsp	salt	1½ tsp
½ tsp	dried sage	¾ tsp
1⅓ cups	bread flour	2 cups
⅔ cup	semolina flour	1 cup
1½ tsp	yeast	2¼ tsp

METHOD

Put ingredients in bread pan in order suggested by your bread machine instructions. Set for white bread, medium crust. Press Start

To toast sesame seeds: put seeds in a small, dry skillet over medium heat. Stir or shake the pan frequently to stop seeds from scorching. Let seeds cool before using.

To roast sweet red bell peppers: cut each pepper into 3 or 4 nearly flat pieces. Place on broiler pan or doubled sheet of aluminum foil. Cook under the broiler until skin turns black and blisters. The pieces won't cook evenly; remove each piece when it is done. As you remove each piece, put it in a bag or foil envelope to steam for 10 minutes, then peel off skin.

If you add the peppers at the beginning of the kneading, in combination with yellow semolina flour they will turn the bread orange. They will also release more moisture into the bread. If you add the peppers late in the kneading, you may need to add another tablespoon of milk. You may use bottled roasted red

DATE GRANOLA BREAD

The variety of granolas available is tremendous. Different types can entirely change the character of the bread. Other than additions like dried fruits and nuts, the biggest difference is in sweetness. This bread, served untoasted with butter, was a favorite with the friends who tried many of my experiments.

1 lb LOAF	INGREDIENTS	1½ lb LOAF
½ cup	water	¾ cup
¼ cup	milk	6 tbsp
1 tbsp	vegetable oil	1½ tbsp
1 tbsp	honey	1½ tbsp
½ tsp	cinnamon	¾ tsp
1 tsp	salt	1½ tsp
½ cup	granola	¾ cup
1¼ cups	bread flour	1⅞ cups
½ cup	whole-wheat flour	¾ cup
1½ tsp	yeast	2¼ tsp
⅓ cup	chopped dates	½ cup

METHOD

Put all ingredients except dates in bread pan in order suggested by your bread machine instructions. Set for whole-wheat bread, medium crust. Press Start. Add dates after first kneading or when machine beeps to add fruit.

This recipe is based on a basic, not-too-sweet granola. You can adjust the amount of honey in the recipe if you're starting with a particularly sweet granola, substitute other fruit, or add nuts. Omit the cinnamon if the granola is already spiced.

SWEET POTATO BREAD

Sweet potato bread has its roots in the southern United States. It has a delicate flavor and pale orange color, but is not a sweet bread. Serve it as an accompaniment to soup or salad, or top it with melted cheese.

1 lb LOAF	INGREDIENTS	1½ lb LOAF
⅔ cup	cooked, mashed sweet potatoes	1 cup
6 tbsp	milk	9 tbsp
2 tbsp	butter	3 tbsp
2 tbsp	sugar	3 tbsp
1 tsp	salt	1½ tsp
2 cups	bread flour	3 cups
2 tsp	yeast	1 tbsp

METHOD

Put ingredients in bread pan in order suggested by your bread machine instructions. Set for whole-wheat bread, medium crust.

You may use canned sweet potatoes for this recipe, but only if there is no sugar or syrup added. Otherwise, bake or boil sweet potatoes and mash them without any additions. The amount of milk needed may vary slightly depending on the water content of the sweet potatoes.

RIGHT Sweet Potato Bread

5

Fruit Breads

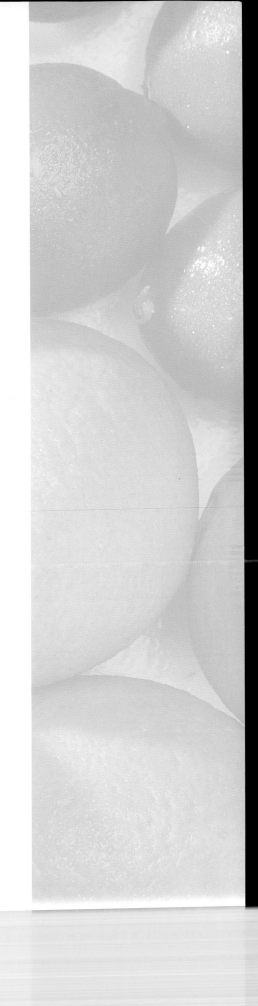

102

Buttermilk Fruit Bread

103

Tropical Pineapple Bread

104

Oatmeal Raisin Bread

105

Pineapple Orange Bran Bread

105

Coconut Date Bread

106

Pear Whole-wheat Bread

108

Sweet Potato Apple Pecan Bread

109

Date-nut Wheat Bread

110

Pumpkin Pecan Bread

111

Cherry Hazelnut Bread

112

Cinnamon Raisin Bread

112

Laura's Ginger Applesauce Bread

113

Mango Macadamia Nut Bread

114

Trail Mix Bread

114

Apricot Graham Bread

116

Pear Bread

117

Cranberry Orange Bread

118

California Almond Fig Bread

118

Almond Poppyseed Bread

119

Orange Cumin Bread

120

Apricot Pecan Anadama Bread

121

Apple-Cranberry Graham Bread

BUTTERMILK FRUIT BREAD

This is a light whole-wheat buttermilk bread with dried fruit and a pinch of cinnamon for flavor. Use any combination of dried fruit, including peaches, apricots, cherries, raisins, and figs.

1 lb LOAF	INGREDIENTS	1½ lb LOAF
½ cup	buttermilk	⅞ cup
1	egg	1
2 tbsp	butter	3 tbsp
2 tbsp	sugar	3 tbsp
½ tsp	salt	¾ tsp
½ tsp	baking soda	½ tsp
½ tsp	cinnamon	¾ tsp
1½ cups	bread flour	2¼ cups
½ cup	whole-wheat flour	¾ cup
1½ tsp	yeast	2¼ tsp
⅓ cup	coarsely chopped dried fruit	½ cup

METHOD

Put all ingredients except fruit in bread pan in order suggested by your bread machine instructions. Set for whole-wheat bread, medium crust. Press Start. Add fruit after the first kneading or when the machine beeps that it's time to add fruit.

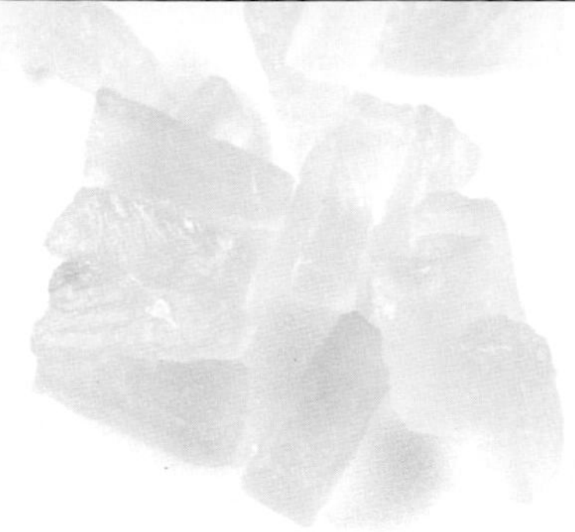

TROPICAL PINEAPPLE BREAD

Candied pineapple sweetens this bread, which is also flavored with coconut, nutmeg, and ginger. It is delicious toasted and spread with cream cheese.

1 lb LOAF	INGREDIENTS	1½ lb LOAF
½ cup	water	¾ cup
¼ cup	milk	6 tbsp
2 tbsp	butter	3 tbsp
2 tbsp	honey	3 tbsp
¼ tsp	ground ginger	½ tsp
¼ tsp	nutmeg	½ tsp
½ tsp	salt	¾ tsp
½ cup	whole-wheat flour	¾ cup
1½ cups	bread flour	2¼ cups
1½ tsp	yeast	2¼ tsp
⅓ cup	diced sugared pineapple	½ cup
¼ cup	grated coconut	6 tbsp
¼ cup	chopped macadamia nuts	6 tbsp

METHOD

Put all but last three ingredients in bread pan in order suggested by your bread machine instructions. Add about half the pineapple, which will be cut into bits by the kneading. Set for white bread, medium crust. Press Start. Add remaining pineapple, coconut, and nuts at beeper or after first kneading.

OATMEAL RAISIN BREAD

This is a hearty breakfast bread.

1lb LOAF	INGREDIENTS	1½lb LOAF
½ cup	very hot water	¾ cup
½ cup	rolled oats	¾ cup
½ cup	milk	¾ cup
1 tbsp	butter	1½ tbsp
2 tbsp	brown sugar	3 tbsp
1 tsp	cinnamon	1½ tsp
1 tsp	salt	1½ tsp
1⅔ cups	bread flour	2½ cups
2 tsp	yeast	1 tbsp
⅓ cup	raisins	½ cup

METHOD

Put oats and hot water in bread machine pan and stir. Let sit at least 10 minutes.

Put remaining ingredients in bread pan in order suggested by your bread machine instructions. Set for white bread, medium crust. Press Start.

After about 15 minutes or when the beeper signals time to add fruit, add raisins.

PINEAPPLE ORANGE BRAN BREAD

This bread, which uses dried candied pineapple, is moist and slightly sweet.
It's good just plain. Use All-Bran or Fiber One, not bran flakes.

1lb LOAF	INGREDIENTS	1½lb LOAF
5 tbsp	water	½ cup
½ cup	milk	¾ cup
1 tbsp	molasses	1½ tbsp
2 tbsp	butter	3 tbsp
1 tsp	grated orange zest	1½ tsp
1 tsp	salt	1½ tsp
⅓ cup	bran cereal	½ cup
1 cup	bread flour	1½ cups
¾ cup	whole-wheat flour	1 cup + 3 tbsp
1½ tsp	yeast	2¼ tsp
¼ cup	chopped candied pineapple	6 tbsp

METHOD

Put all ingredients except pineapple in bread pan in order suggested by your bread machine instructions. Set for whole-wheat bread, medium crust. Press Start. After about 15 minutes or when the beeper signals time to add fruit, add pineapple.

COCONUT DATE BREAD

Coconut, dates and nuts give this bread a tropical flavor.

1lb LOAF	INGREDIENTS	1½lb LOAF
1	egg	2
3 tbsp	water	2½ tbsp
⅓ cup	milk	½ cup
1 tbsp	butter	1½ tbsp
2 tbsp	sugar	3 tbsp
1 tsp	ground allspice	1½ tsp
1 tsp	salt	1½ tsp
2 tbsp	wheat germ	3 tbsp
1 cup	bread flour	1½ cups
1 cup	whole-wheat flour	1½ cups
1½ tsp	yeast	2¼ tsp
¼ cup	chopped dates	6 tbsp
¼ cup	sweetened flaked	6 tbsp

METHOD

Put all but last three ingredients in bread pan in order suggested by your bread machine instructions. Set for whole-wheat bread, medium crust. Press Start. After about 15 minutes or when the beeper signals time to add fruit, add the dates, coconut and nuts.

PEAR WHOLE-WHEAT BREAD

This is a good whole-wheat bread for breakfast, with a faint taste of pears, and texture added by the bulgur.

1lb LOAF	INGREDIENTS	1½lb LOAF
½ cup	puréed pear (see method)	¾ cup
¼ cup	bulgur	6 tbsp
2 cups	water	2 cups
5 tbsp	pear liquid (see method)	7½ tbsp
2 tbsp	powdered milk	3 tbsp
1 tbsp	butter	1½ tbsp
1 tbsp	honey	1½ tbsp
1 tsp	salt	1½ tsp
1 cup	bread flour	1½ cups
1 cup	whole-wheat flour	1½ cups
2 tsp	yeast	1 tbsp

METHOD

Make the pear purée by peeling and coring 3 ripe pears for the smaller loaf, 4 or 5 pears for the larger one. Cut each pear into several pieces and put in a small saucepan with 1 or 2 tablespoons water. Start cooking over very low heat. The pears will quickly start releasing their own juices, and no more water will be needed. Increase to medium heat. Cook the pears, stirring frequently, until they are very soft. Then drain off as much liquid as you can, and save. If necessary, purée the pears in a blender or food processor, but mashing them with a fork may do the job. Then measure the amount needed in the recipe. Let cool.

Put the bulgur wheat in a small pan with 2 cups water. Bring to a boil and let boil for 6 minutes. Remove from heat and drain. Let cool 15 minutes. Blot with paper towel to absorb any excess moisture.

Put puréed pear, bulgur, measured pear liquid, and remaining ingredients in bread pan in order suggested by your bread machine instructions. Set for whole-wheat bread, medium crust. Press Start.

The stiffness of the dough may vary, depending on the liquid content of the cooked pears. Watch the dough while it is kneading and add a little flour, 1 tablespoon at a time, if it is too soft. Add water, 1 teaspoon at a time, if the dough is too stiff.

SWEET POTATO APPLE PECAN BREAD

This bread is slightly sweet, enhanced by the spices, dried apples and pecans in it.
It is best toasted or plain with sweet butter, but would also be good
for cream cheese sandwiches.

1lb LOAF	INGREDIENTS	1½lb LOAF
⅓ cup	milk	½ cup
⅔ cup	puréed, cooked sweet potato	1 cup
2 tbsp	butter	3 tbsp
2 tbsp	honey	3 tbsp
1 tsp	salt	1½ tsp
½ tsp	cinnamon	¾ tsp
¼ tsp	ground cloves	¼ tsp
2 cups	bread flour	3 cups
1½ tsp	yeast	2¼ tsp
¼ cup	chopped dried apples	6 tbsp
⅓ cup	chopped pecans	½ cup

METHOD

Put all ingredients except apples and nuts in bread pan in order suggested by your bread machine instructions. Set for white bread, medium crust. Press Start.

The stiffness of the dough may vary, depending on the liquid content of the sweet potato purée. Watch the dough while it is kneading and add a little flour, 1 tablespoon at a time, if it is too soft. Add water, 1 teaspoon at a time, if the dough is too stiff.

After about 15 minutes or when the beeper signals time to add fruit, add apples and pecans.

DATE-NUT WHEAT BREAD

This is a dense bread with lots of texture added by the bulgur, dates, and walnuts.
The dates also give it just a touch of sweetness. Use it for toast or with cream cheese.

1lb LOAF	INGREDIENTS	1½lb LOAF
¼ cup	bulgur	6 tbsp
2¼ cups	water	2 cups + 6 tbsp
⅓ cup	milk	½ cup
1 tbsp	honey	1½ tbsp
2 tbsp	butter	3 tbsp
1 tsp	salt	1½ tsp
½ tsp	cinnamon	¾ tsp
1 cup	whole-wheat flour	1½ cups
1 cup	bread flour	1½ cups
2 tsp	yeast	1 tbsp
⅓ cup	chopped dates	½ cup
¼ cup	chopped walnuts	6 tbsp

METHOD

Put the bulgur in a small pan with 2 cups water. Bring to a boil and let boil for 6 minutes. Remove from heat and drain. Let cool 15 minutes. Blot with paper towel to absorb excess moisture.

Put cooled bulgur, remaining water, and all other ingredients except dates and walnuts in bread pan in order suggested by your bread machine instructions. Set for whole-wheat bread, medium crust. Press Start. After about 15 minutes or when the beeper signals time to add fruit, add dates and walnuts.

PUMPKIN PECAN BREAD

*This is not the traditional sweet, dense, baking powder pumpkin bread, but
a light and slightly sweet yeast bread that is flavored with pumpkin, pecans,
and spices. Eat it warm with butter or make turkey sandwiches with it.*

1 lb LOAF	INGREDIENTS	1½ lb LOAF
⅓ cup	milk	½ cup
¾ cup	puréed pumpkin	1¼ cups
2 tbsp	butter	3 tbsp
3 tbsp	sugar	4½ tbsp
½ tsp	salt	¾ tsp
1 tsp	cinnamon	1½ tsp
½ tsp	ground ginger	¾ tsp
¼ tsp	ground cloves	¼ tsp
½ cup	chopped pecans	¾ cup
2 cups	bread flour	3 cups
2 tsp	yeast	1 tbsp

METHOD

Put ingredients in bread pan in order suggested by your
bread machine instructions. Set for white bread, light
crust. Press Start.

The amount of milk needed may vary slightly, depending
on the water content of the pumpkin. Be sure you are
using pure pumpkin, not pumpkin pie filling.

CHERRY HAZELNUT BREAD

This is a light whole-wheat bread, made special by the addition of tart dried cherries and toasted hazelnuts. It is not a sweet bread, so it goes with meals.

1 lb LOAF	INGREDIENTS	1½ lb LOAF
½ cup	milk	⅞ cup
1	egg	1
2 tbsp	butter	3 tbsp
2 tbsp	sugar	3 tbsp
½ tsp	salt	¾ tsp
1½ cups	bread flour	2¼ cups
½ cup	whole-wheat flour	¾ cup
1½ tsp	yeast	2¼ tsp
¼ cup	dried cherries	6 tbsp
3 tbsp	chopped toasted hazelnuts	4½ tbsp

METHOD

Put all ingredients except cherries and hazelnuts in bread pan in order suggested by your bread machine instructions. Set for whole-wheat bread, medium crust. Press Start. Add cherries and hazelnuts after the first kneading, or when the machine signals to add fruit.

Note: To toast shelled hazelnuts, spread them in a single layer on an ungreased baking sheet. Bake them in a 350°F oven for 10 minutes, stirring two or three times. Allow the nuts to cool, wrap them in a coarse towel, and rub them together to remove the papery membrane.

CINNAMON RAISIN BREAD

*This is a light, slightly sweet whole-wheat bread. It is good for toast,
and delicious with apple or pumpkin butter.*

1 lb LOAF	INGREDIENTS	1½ lb LOAF
½ cup	water	¾ cup
¼ cup	milk	6 tbsp
2 tbsp	butter	3 tbsp
3 tbsp	brown sugar	4½ tbsp
½ tsp	salt	¾ tsp
2 tsp	cinnamon	1 tbsp
1½ cups	bread flour	2¼ cups
½ cup	whole-wheat flour	¾ cup
2 tsp	yeast	1 tbsp
⅓ cup	raisins	½ cup

METHOD

Put all ingredients except raisins in bread pan in order suggested by your bread machine instructions. Set for whole-wheat bread, medium crust. Press Start. Add raisins after the first kneading, or when the machine signals that it is time to add fruit.

If you want whole raisins, add them after the first kneading. Add them at the beginning if you want a darker color and an overall sweeter, raisiny taste. If your raisins are so dry that you plump them up in hot water, blot every bit of water off them before adding them. Wet raisins will alter the flour/liquid balance.

LAURA'S GINGER APPLESAUCE BREAD

*The flavor of ginger and apples is just right in this bread, tasty but not
overwhelming. Graham flour gives it good texture.*

1 lb LOAF	INGREDIENTS	1½ lb LOAF
⅓ cup	water	½ cup
½ cup	unsweetened applesauce	¾ cup
2 tbsp	powdered milk	3 tbsp
1 tbsp	butter	1½ tbsp
2 tbsp	molasses	3 tbsp
1 tsp	ground ginger	1½ tsp
½ tsp	salt	¾ tsp
1 cup	bread flour	1½ cups
1 cup	graham flour	1½ cups
1½ tsp	yeast	2¼ tsp

METHOD

Put ingredients in bread pan in order suggested by your bread machine instructions. Set for whole-wheat bread, medium crust. Press Start.

The amount of water needed will depend on the water content of the applesauce. If the applesauce is runny, simmer it on the stovetop to evaporate excess water. Check the dough during kneading to see if the amount of flour or water needs to be adjusted.

MANGO MACADAMIA NUT BREAD

With its tropical flavor, this bread goes well with a fruited chicken salad sandwich.

1 lb LOAF	INGREDIENTS	1½ lb LOAF
⅓ cup	old-fashioned rolled oats	½ cup
¼ cup	boiling water	6 tbsp
½ cup	puréed mango	¾ cup
¼ cup	milk	6 tbsp
1 tbsp	butter	1½ tbsp
2 tsp	sugar	1 tbsp
½ tsp	salt	¾ tsp
¼ tsp	ground ginger	½ tsp
¼ tsp	nutmeg	½ tsp
1¾ cups	bread flour	2⅔ cups
2 tsp	yeast	1 tbsp
¼ cup	chopped macadamia nuts	6 tbsp

METHOD

Put the oats in bread machine pan and pour the boiling water over them. Stir so all the oats are wet. Let sit at least 15 minutes. Add all the remaining ingredients except the nuts. Set for white bread, medium crust. Press Start. Check the dough after about 10 minutes. Depending on the water content of the mango, the dough may need a little more milk or flour. Add the nuts after the first kneading or when the machine signals to add fruit or nuts.

TRAIL MIX BREAD

Trail mix is a kitchen-sink sort of concoction made up of any kind of dried fruit, seeds, or nuts, from the ordinary to the exotic, and may be sweetened with bits of coconut, or other goodies. Likewise, Trail Mix Bread is a kitchen-sink sort of bread.

1 lb LOAF	INGREDIENTS	1½ lb LOAF
½ cup	water	¾ cup
¼ cup	milk	6 tbsp
2 tbsp	vegetable oil	3 tbsp
2 tbsp	honey	3 tbsp
1 tsp	salt	1½ tsp
1⅓ cups	bread flour	2 cups
⅔ cup	whole-wheat flour	1 cup
1½ tsp	yeast	2¼ tsp
½ cup	trail mix	¾ cup

METHOD

Put all ingredients except trail mix in bread pan in order suggested by your bread machine instructions. Set for whole-wheat bread, medium crust. Press Start. Add trail mix at the beeper or after first kneading.

If the only trail mix you can find is a mix of raisins and sunflower seeds, doctor it with dates, dried apricots, dried cherries, pecans, or cashews. Coarsely chop whole nuts such as almonds. Avoid using chocolate in the trail mix as it tends to burn in a bread machine.

APRICOT GRAHAM BREAD

Dried apricots and molasses give this bread a hint of sweetness, while the graham flour gives it a slightly chewy texture. It's a delicious breakfast bread that also goes well with chicken or cream cheese sandwiches.

1 lb LOAF	INGREDIENTS	1½ lb LOAF
⅔ cup	water	1 cup
1 tbsp	vegetable oil	1½ tbsp
2 tbsp	molasses	3 tbsp
⅓ cup	coarsely chopped dried apricots	½ cup
2 tbsp	powdered milk	3 tbsp
½ tsp	salt	¾ tsp
1 cup	bread flour	1½ cups
1 cup	graham flour	1½ cups
1½ tsp	yeast	2¼ tsp

METHOD

Put ingredients in bread pan in order suggested by your bread machine instructions. Set for whole-wheat bread, medium crust. Press Start.

RIGHT Trail Mix Bread

PEAR BREAD

*This is based on a bread made in the French countryside amid pear orchards.
It has a delicate, sweet flavor of pears. It is a nice tea or breakfast bread,
or can be used in mildly flavored sandwiches such as cream
cheese and cucumber.*

1 lb LOAF	INGREDIENTS	1½ lb LOAF
½ cup	pear purée	¾ cup
about 3 tbsp	pear liquid or water	4–5 tbsp
2 tsp	honey	1 tbsp
2 tbsp	butter	3 tbsp
½ tsp	salt	¾ tsp
½ tsp	ground ginger	¾ tsp
½ tsp	nutmeg	¾ tsp
2 cups	bread flour	3 cups
1½ tsp	yeast	2¼ tsp

METHOD

Make the pear purée by peeling and coring 3 pears for
the smaller recipe, 4 or 5 pears for the larger one. Cut
each pear in several pieces and put in a small saucepan
with 1 or 2 tbsp water. Start cooking over very low heat.
The pears will quickly start releasing their own juices,
and no more water will be needed. Increase to medium
heat. Cook the pears until they are very soft, about 10
minutes. Then drain off as much liquid as you can,
saving the liquid. Put the pears in a blender or food
processor and purée.

Measure out the required amount of purée. Put it and
all other ingredients except pear liquid in bread pan in
order suggested by your bread machine instructions.
The amount of liquid needed for the bread will depend
on the liquid in the purée, so you'll need to watch the
dough for the first few minutes, adding pear liquid (or
plain water) until it reaches the proper consistency –
neither stiff nor too soft. Set for white bread, medium
crust. Press Start. Once you have added the liquid, the
bread does not need any further attention until it is
baked.

CRANBERRY ORANGE BREAD

This bread is flavored with cranberries and orange peel, but don't save it only for the holidays. It is slightly sweet, but is not sweet enough to be a dessert bread. Use it for toast or sandwiches of turkey or pork.

1 lb LOAF	INGREDIENTS	1½ lb LOAF
½ cup	water	¾ cup
2 tbsp	butter	3 tbsp
3 tbsp	sugar	4½ tbsp
½ tsp	salt	¾ tsp
2 tsp	grated orange peel	1 tbsp
½ tsp	nutmeg	¾ tsp
⅔ cup	cranberries	1 cup
½ cup	whole-wheat flour	¾ cup
1½ cups	bread flour	2¼ cups
2 tsp	yeast	1 tbsp

METHOD

Put ingredients in bread pan in order suggested by your bread machine instructions. Set for white bread, medium crust. Press Start.

You may use fresh or frozen cranberries, but allow frozen cranberries to thaw before adding them to the dough. If you add whole cranberries at the same time as the other ingredients, the kneading action of the bread machine will chop them to the right size. Although the dough may initially seem dry, it will gain some liquid from the cranberries.

CALIFORNIA ALMOND FIG BREAD

The additions to this yogurt bread – almonds and figs – come from California's Central Valley. It is not a sweet bread, although the figs give it a hint of sweetness.

1 lb LOAF	INGREDIENTS	1½ lb LOAF
½ cup	plain yogurt	¾ cup
¼ cup	water	6 tbsp
1 tbsp	vegetable oil	1½ tbsp
2 tbsp	honey	3 tbsp
½ tsp	salt	¾ tsp
3 tbsp	oat bran	4½ tbsp
2 cups	bread flour	3 cups
1½ tsp	yeast	2¼ tsp
⅓ cup	coarsely chopped figs	½ cup
3 tbsp	slivered blanched almonds	4½ tbsp

METHOD

Put all ingredients except figs and almonds in bread pan in order suggested by your bread machine instructions. Set for white bread, medium crust. Press Start. Add figs and almonds after the first kneading, or when the machine signals that it is time to add fruit.

ALMOND POPPYSEED BREAD

This is a light, barely sweet bread, with oatmeal adding texture. It is a good bread for breakfast or a snack, and not at all like those gummy, overly sweet muffins.

1 lb LOAF	INGREDIENTS	1½ lb LOAF
1	egg	1
½ cup	milk	⅞ cup
2 tbsp	butter	3 tbsp
2 tbsp	sugar	3 tbsp
1 tsp	almond extract	1½ tsp
2 tbsp	poppy seeds	3 tbsp
½ tsp	salt	¾ tsp
⅓ cup	old-fashioned rolled oats	½ cup
1¾ cups	bread flour	2⅔ cups
1½ tsp	yeast	2¼ tsp
¼ cup	slivered almonds	6 tbsp

METHOD

Put all ingredients except almonds in bread pan in order suggested by your bread machine instructions. Set for white bread, medium crust. Press Start. Add almonds at the beeper or after the first kneading.

ORANGE CUMIN BREAD

This light whole-wheat bread is slightly sweet and flavored with orange and cumin, a pungent spice frequently used in Mexican, Middle Eastern, Asian, and Mediterranean cooking. Try this bread with chicken or fish.

1 lb LOAF	INGREDIENTS	1½ lb LOAF
½ cup	milk	¾ cup
¼ cup	water	6 tbsp
2 tbsp	vegetable oil	3 tbsp
3 tbsp	sugar	4½ tbsp
1 tbsp	grated orange peel	1½ tbsp
¾ tsp	ground cumin	1¼ tsp
1 tsp	salt	1½ tsp
2 tbsp	cornmeal	3 tbsp
1½ cups	bread flour	2¼ cups
½ cup	whole-wheat flour	¾ cup
1½ tsp	yeast	2¼ tsp

METHOD

Put ingredients in bread pan in order suggested by your bread machine instructions. Set for whole-wheat bread, medium crust. Press Start.

APRICOT PECAN ANADAMA BREAD

Anadama bread is an old New England hearth bread traditionally made with cornmeal and molasses. This recipe dresses it up with dried apricots and pecans, and makes a delicious breakfast or luncheon bread.

1lb LOAF	INGREDIENTS	1½lb LOAF
½ cup	water	¾ cup
¼ cup	milk	6 tbsp
1 tbsp	butter	1½ tbsp
2 tbsp	molasses	3 tbsp
1 tsp	salt	1½ tsp
¼ cup	cornmeal	6 tbsp
2 cups	bread flour	3 cups
1½ tsp	yeast	2¼ tsp
⅓ cup	chopped dried apricots	½ cup
¼ cup	chopped pecans	6 tbsp

METHOD

Put all ingredients except apricots and pecans in bread pan in order suggested by your bread machine instructions. Set for white bread, medium crust. Press Start. After about 15 minutes or when the beeper signals time to add fruit, add apricots and pecans.

APPLE-CRANBERRY GRAHAM BREAD

*Delicately flavored with applesauce and a hint of spice, balanced by the tang
of dried cranberries, this bread is given its soft but slightly chewy texture
by graham flour.*

1lb LOAF	INGREDIENTS	1½lb LOAF
⅓ cup	water	½ cup
⅔ cup	unsweetened applesauce	1 cup
1 tbsp	vegetable oil	1½ tbsp
1 tbsp	molasses	1½ tbsp
2 tbsp	powdered milk	3 tbsp
½ tsp	cinnamon	¾ tsp
½ tsp	ginger	¾ tsp
½ tsp	salt	¾ tsp
1 cup	bread flour	1½ cups
1 cup	graham flour	1½ cups
1½ tsp	yeast	2¼ tsp
⅓ cup	dried, sweetened cranberries	½ cup

METHOD

Put ingredients except cranberries in bread pan in order suggested by your bread machine instructions. Set for whole-wheat bread, medium crust. Press Start. After about 15 minutes of kneading or when the beeper signals time to add fruit, add cranberries.

The stiffness of the dough may vary, depending on the liquid content of the applesauce. Watch the dough while it is kneading and add a little flour, 1 tablespoon at a time, if it is too soft. Add water, 1 teaspoon at a time, if the dough is too stiff.

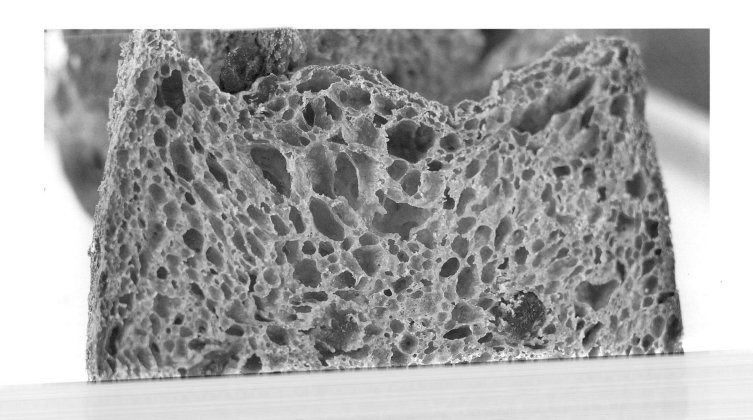

6

Oven-Baked Breads, Rolls, and Breadsticks

CROISSANTS

This is a much simplified version of the flaky layered croissant that requires so much time and patience to make. It is very buttery, but the butter is kneaded into the dough with the other ingredients instead of being folded in afterwards. It's very important that the butter is at room temperature – not melted – when it is used.

MAKES 16	INGREDIENTS	MAKES 24
½ cup	water	¾ cup
2 tbsp	powdered milk	3 tbsp
½ cup	butter	¾ cup
1 tbsp	sugar	1½ tbsp
1 tsp	salt	1½ tsp
2 cups	bread flour	3 cups
2 tsp	yeast	1 tbsp

GLAZE

1 egg
pinch of salt

METHOD

Put all ingredients except glaze in bread pan in order suggested by your bread machine instructions. Set for white bread, dough stage. Press Start.

Lightly butter two baking sheets.

When dough is ready, remove from bread machine and punch down. Cut the smaller recipe in two pieces, the larger recipe into three pieces. Let dough rest 5 minutes. Roll each piece of dough into a circle about 10 inches in diameter and ⅛ inch thick. To get the dough this thin, you may need to let it relax a little during the rolling.

Cut each circle into eight equal wedges. Take each wedge and roll it one more time with the rolling pin to flatten it. Starting at the wide end of the wedge, roll up the dough toward the point, stretching the dough slightly as you go. Place, with tip under the roll, on baking sheet. Pull ends toward front so the roll forms a crescent.

Make glaze by beating egg and salt together with a fork. Brush croissants with glaze. Cover loosely and set in a warm place to rise until doubled, about 1 hour. Brush again with glaze. Bake in a preheated 375°F oven until golden brown, 20 to 25 minutes.

CRISP BREADSTICKS

These thin breadsticks will keep for several days if they are stored in an airtight container.

MAKES 24	INGREDIENTS	MAKES 36
⅔ cup	water	1 cup
¼ cup	vegetable oil	6 tbsp
2 tsp	sugar	1 tbsp
1 tsp	salt	1½ tsp
2 cups	bread flour	3 cups
2 tsp	yeast	1 tbsp
about 2 tbsp	vegetable oil	about 3 tbsp
1	egg white	1
2 tbsp	water	2 tbsp

sesame or poppy seeds or coarse salt, optional

METHOD

Put all but last three ingredients in bread pan in order suggested by your bread machine instructions. Set for white bread, dough stage. Press Start.

Grease 2 or 3 baking sheets.

When dough is ready, remove from bread pan and punch down. Cut smaller batch into 24 pieces, larger batch into 36 pieces. Roll each piece between your palms to form a very skinny rope, about 8 inches long. Place bread sticks 1 inch apart on baking sheets. Brush lightly with oil. Cover loosely and set in a warm place to rise 20 to 25 minutes.

Preheat oven to 350°F. Make wash of egg white and 2 tbsp water. Brush egg wash lightly on bread sticks. Sprinkle with seeds or salt, if desired. Bake until golden brown, about 25 minutes.

SOFT BREADSTICKS

These soft bread sticks do not keep well, but they are delicious still warm from the oven. Sprinkle them with sesame or poppy seeds or coarse salt.

MAKES 20	INGREDIENTS	MAKES 30
10 tbsp	water	1 cup
1	egg, separated	1
2 tbsp	vegetable oil	3 tbsp
2 tsp	sugar	1 tbsp
1 tsp	salt	1½ tsp
2 cups	bread flour	3 cups
1½ tsp	yeast	2¼ tsp
2 tbsp	water	2 tbsp

sesame or poppy seeds or coarse salt, optional

METHOD

Separate the egg and put the yolk in the bread pan. Save the white for glaze. Put remaining ingredients except last 2 tbsp water and seeds in bread pan in order suggested by your bread machine instructions. Set for white bread, dough stage. Press Start.

Grease 2 or 3 baking sheets. Make a wash of the egg white and 2 tbsp water. Preheat oven to 350°F.

When dough is ready, remove from bread machine and punch down. Cut the dough into 20 pieces for the smaller recipe, 30 pieces for the larger recipe. Roll each piece between your palms to form a rope about 6 inches long. Place breadsticks on baking sheet about 1½ inches apart. Brush with egg wash. Sprinkle with seeds or salt, if desired.

Bake breadsticks until golden, 20 to 25 minutes.

HAMBURGER BUNS AND HOT DOG ROLLS

Baking your own hamburger buns or hot dog rolls is as easy as making simple dinner rolls.

MAKES 6	INGREDIENTS	MAKES 9
1	egg	1
½ cup	milk	⅞ cup
3 tbsp	butter	4½ tbsp
2 tbsp	sugar	3 tbsp
½ tsp	salt	¾ tsp
2 cups	bread flour	3 cups
2 tsp	yeast	1 tbsp
2 tbsp	milk	3 tbsp

sesame seeds, optional

METHOD

Put all ingredients except 2 or 3 tbsp milk and sesame seeds in bread pan in order suggested by your bread machine instructions. Set for white bread, dough stage. Press Start.

When dough is ready, remove from bread machine and punch down. Cut smaller recipe into 6 equal pieces, the larger recipe into 9 pieces. Let dough rest 5 minutes while you butter one or two baking sheets. For hamburger buns, roll each piece into a ball and flatten it to form a patty about 3 inches wide and ½ inch thick. For hot dog buns, roll each piece into a 6-inch rope and flatten to ½ inch thickness. Place rolls on baking sheet. Cover loosely and set in a warm place to rise for 20 minutes. Preheat oven to 400°F.

Lightly brush tops of rolls with milk and sprinkle with sesame seeds, if desired. Bake to 12 to 15 minutes, until a skewer inserted in roll comes out clean.

BAGELS

Dense and chewy, bagels are a delight when they are split and toasted and served with butter or cream cheese. They also make delicious sandwiches. You can experiment by adding chopped sautéed onions, or raisins and cinnamon, to the dough.

MAKES 8-10	INGREDIENTS	MAKES 12-15
1	egg	1
½ cup	milk	1 cup
1 tbsp	vegetable oil	1½ tbsp
2 tsp	sugar	1 tbsp
½ tsp	salt	¼ tsp
2 cups	bread flour	3 cups
2 tsp	yeast	1 tbsp
1 tbsp	sugar	1 tbsp
1	egg white	1
2 tsp	water	2 tsp

sesame or poppy seeds or coarse salt

METHOD

Put all but last four ingredients in bread pan in order suggested by your bread machine instructions. Set for white bread, dough stage. Press Start.

When dough is ready, remove from bread machine and punch down. Cut smaller recipe into 8 to 10 equal pieces, the larger recipe into 12 to 15 pieces. Roll each piece between your palms to form a thin rope, about 8 inches long with tapered ends. Bring ends together to form a circle, with the tapered ends overlapping. With moistened fingers, pinch or lightly knead the joined ends so the circle is securely fastened, or it will come apart later.

Set the bagels in a warm place to rise and cover them loosely. They should rise for 15 minutes. Preheat oven to 400°F. While they are rising, bring about 2 quarts of water to boil in a saucepan.
Add 1 tbsp sugar. When the bagels have risen for 15 minutes, drop one or two at a time into the boiling water, handling them as gently as possible so they do not deflate. They will rise to the surface of the water and swell up. Let them cook 1 minute, then turn them over and let them cook 3 minutes longer.

Remove bagels, let drain over the water, and place on an ungreased baking sheet. Beat egg white with water and brush over bagels. Sprinkle with sesame or poppy seeds or coarse salt. Bake until golden, 20 to 25 minutes.

FOUGASSE

*Fougasse is a flatbread made in southern France that is similar to foccacio but is
cut prior to baking. This recipe is more elaborate than a basic fougasse. It is a good
appetizer or an accompaniment to soup or salad.*

1lb LOAF	INGREDIENTS	1½lb LOAF
2 slices	bacon	3 slices
⅔ cup	water	1 cup
2 tbsp	olive oil	3 tbsp
2 tsp	sugar	1 tbsp
1 tsp	salt	1½ tsp
1 tsp	fine chopped rosemary, fresh or dry	1½ tsp
2 cups	bread flour	3 cups
1½ tsp	yeast	2¼ tsp
⅓ cup	chopped onion	½ cup
1 tbsp	olive oil	1 tbsp
3–4 tbsp	grated Parmesan cheese	4–5 tbsp

METHOD

Dice bacon. Fry until crisp. Drain and cool. Put bacon
and next seven ingredients in bread pan in order
suggested by your bread machine instructions. Set for
dough. Press Start. While dough is rising, sauté onions
in remaining olive oil. Set aside to cool.

When dough is ready, punch it down on a lightly
floured board. Let it rest a few minutes. Gently knead in
the onions. Then roll it into an oval, about ½ inch
thick. With a sharp knife, make several diagonal cuts in
the bread, and stretch the dough so the cuts open wide.
Sprinkle cornmeal on a baking sheet. Put the dough on
the sheet. Sprinkle with the cheese. Cover with lightly
buttered wax paper or plastic wrap. Put in a warm place
to rise for 45 minutes. Bake bread in a preheated 375°F
oven until lightly browned, about 20 to 25 minutes.

BRAIDED BRIOCHE

This pretty braided loaf uses a traditional brioche recipe, rich with eggs and butter.
It is full of flavor and good simply plain, but it can be buttered or used for toast.

1lb LOAF	INGREDIENTS	1½lb LOAF
¼ cup	milk	6 tbsp
2	eggs	3
6 tbsp	butter, at room temperature	½ cup + 1 tbsp
3 tbsp	sugar	4½ tbsp
½ tsp	salt	¾ tsp
2 cups	bread flour	3 cups
1½ tsp	yeast	2¼ tsp

TOPPING

1 egg yolk
1 tsp water
2–3 tbsp sliced almonds

METHOD

Put dough ingredients in bread pan in order suggested by your bread machine instructions. Set for dough. Press Start.

When dough is ready, punch it down on a lightly floured board. Let it rest a few minutes. Cut it into three pieces. Roll each piece between your hands to form a thin rope, about 15 inches long for the smaller loaf, 18 to 20 inches for the larger. Put the three ropes on a lightly buttered baking sheet. At one end, pinch the three ends together. Then braid loosely, pinching the ends together at the bottom. Make a wash of the egg yolk and water, lightly beating with a fork. Paint the wash on the top of the bread and sprinkle with the almonds.

Cover and let rise 45 to 60 minutes in a warm place. When bread has risen, place in a preheated 350°F oven and bake until the top is golden brown, 30 to 50 minutes.

Walnut Cheese Breadsticks

Toasting the walnuts boosts the flavor of these crisp breadsticks. Enjoy them with a meal or snack or with a glass of red wine.

MAKES 16–20	INGREDIENTS	MAKES 24–30
¼ cup	finely chopped walnuts	6 tbsp
½ cup + 1 tbsp	water	¾ cup + 2 tbsp
1 tbsp	sugar	1½ tbsp
2 tbsp	vegetable oil	3 tbsp
⅓ cup	grated Cheddar cheese	½ cup
1 tsp	salt	1½ tsp
2 cups	bread flour	3 cups
1½ tsp	yeast	2¼ tsp

EGG WASH

1 egg white
2 tsp water

METHOD

Spread the walnuts on a small baking sheet and put in a preheated 350°F oven for 7 to 12 minutes. Watch closely and stir often until walnuts turn a deeper brown and give off a toasty scent. Let cool.

Put cooled walnuts and remaining dough ingredients in bread pan in order suggested by your bread machine instructions. Set for white bread, dough stage. Press Start.

Grease two or three baking sheets.

When dough is ready, remove from bread pan and punch down. Cut smaller quantity into 16 to 20 pieces, larger into 24 to 30 pieces. Roll each piece between your palms to form a thin rope, about 6 to 8 inches long. Place breadsticks 1 inch apart on baking sheets. Cover loosely and put in a warm place to rise for 20 to 25 minutes.

Beat egg white and water together with a fork. Brush over breadsticks. Bake in a preheated 350°F oven until golden brown, 20 to 25 minutes.

ARMENIAN SESAME ROLLS

The egg dough for these rolls is divided into ropes that are coiled into snails and sprinkled with sesame seeds. Baked to a golden brown, they are an impressive sight at breakfast, tea or dinner.

MAKES 8	**INGREDIENTS**	MAKES 12
1	egg	2
½ cup	milk	⅔ cup
2 tbsp	butter	3 tbsp
3 tbsp	sugar	4½ tbsp
½ tsp	salt	¾ tsp
2 cups	bread flour	3 cups
1½ tsp	yeast	2¼ tsp

TOPPING

1 egg, beaten with a fork
2–3 tbsp sesame seeds

METHOD

Put dough ingredients in bread pan in the

dough stage. Press Start.

When dough is ready, punch it down on a lightly floured board. Let it rest a few minutes. Sprinkle cornmeal on two baking sheets. Cut the dough into 8 pieces for the smaller recipe, 12 pieces for the larger. Roll each piece between your hands until it forms a long, thin rope, 8 to 10 inches long. Beginning at one end, coil the rope around itself like a snail, and pinch the end under the outside of the coil. Put the coils 2 inches apart on the baking sheets.

Brush the tops with the beaten egg and sprinkle generously with sesame seeds. Cover, put in a warm place and let rise 1½ to 2 hours.

PUMPKIN CRANBERRY ROLLS

These are great dinner rolls during the holidays or at any time. The pumpkin flavor is subtle, the dried cranberries add a nice tang, and the rolls are not sweet. They are best served warm.

MAKES 12	INGREDIENTS	MAKES 18
⅔ cup	pumpkin purée	1 cup
1	egg	1 egg + 1 yolk
2 tbsp	powdered milk	3 tbsp
2 tbsp	butter	3 tbsp
2 tbsp	sugar	3 tbsp
1 tsp	salt	1½ tsp
½ tsp	cinnamon	¾ tsp
½ tsp	ground ginger	¾ tsp
¼ tsp	ground cloves	¼ tsp
2 cups	bread flour	3 cups
1½ tsp	yeast	2¼ tsp
⅓ cup	sweetened dried cranberries	½ cup

METHOD

Put all ingredients except cranberries in bread pan in order suggested by your bread machine instructions. Set for white bread, dough stage. Press Start. After about 15 minutes or when the beeper signals time to add fruit, add the cranberries.

Butter muffin tins: 12 cups for the smaller recipe, 18 cups for the larger recipe.

When dough is ready, punch it down and let it rest a few minutes. Cut dough into 12 pieces for the smaller recipe, 18 pieces for the larger. Roll each piece into a ball; it does not have to be perfectly round. Place each ball of dough in a muffin cup. Set in a warm place to rise until doubled in size, 45 to 60 minutes.

When dough is ready, bake in a preheated 350°F oven until a knife or wooden pick inserted in the middle of a roll comes out clean, about 15 minutes.

RYE BREADSTICKS WITH CRACKED PEPPER

Cracked pepper adds zip to these breadsticks, while rosemary – fresh or dried – adds flavor.

MAKES 16–20	INGREDIENTS	MAKES 24–30
⅔ cup	water	1 cup
1 tbsp	sugar	1½ tbsp
2 tbsp	vegetable oil	3 tbsp
2 tsp	finely chopped fresh rosemary	1 tbsp
1 tsp	cracked pepper	1½ tsp
1 tsp	salt	1½ tsp
⅔ cup	rye flour	1 cup
1⅓ cups	bread flour	2 cups
1½ tsp	yeast	2¼ tsp

EGG WASH

1 egg white

2 tsp water

METHOD

Put dough ingredients in bread pan in order suggested by your bread machine instructions. Set for whole-wheat bread, dough stage. Press Start.

Grease two or three baking sheets.

When dough is ready, remove from bread pan and punch down. Cut small quantity into 16 to 20 pieces, larger into 24 to 30 pieces. Roll each piece between your palms to form a thin rope, about 6 to 8 inches long. Place breadsticks 1 inch apart on baking sheets. Cover loosely and put in a warm place to rise for 20 to 25 minutes.

Beat egg white and water together with a fork. Brush over breadsticks. Bake in a preheated 350°F oven until golden brown, 20 to 25 minutes.

ROSEMARY CURRANT BUTTER ROLLS

These buttery whole-wheat dinner rolls demonstrate the surprisingly complementary flavors of currants and rosemary.

MAKES 8–10	INGREDIENTS	MAKES 12–15
1	egg	2
½ cup + 2 tbsp	milk	¾ cup
1 tbsp	sugar	1½ tbsp
2 tbsp	butter	3 tbsp
2 tsp	finely chopped fresh rosemary	1 tbsp
1 tsp	salt	1½ tsp
⅔ cup	whole-wheat flour	1 cup
1⅓ cups	bread flour	2 cups
1½ tsp	yeast	2¼ tsp
⅓ cup	currants	½ cup
1½–2 tbsp	very soft butter	2–3 tbsp

METHOD

Put all ingredients except currants and soft butter in bread pan in order suggested by your bread machine instructions. Set for whole-wheat bread, dough stage. Press Start. After about 15 minutes or when the beeper signals time to add fruit, add currants.

Butter muffin tins: 8 to 10 cups for the smaller recipe, 12 to 15 cups for the larger.

When dough is ready, punch it down on a floured board. Let it rest a few minutes. Roll into a rectangle ⅓ inch thick, squaring off the corners. Spread softened butter over surface. Cut the dough lengthwise into four strips. Stack the four strips, one on top of the other. Trim the uneven ends. Cut through the width of the stack, into 8 to 10 pieces for the smaller recipe, 12 to 15 pieces for the larger. Put each piece in a muffin cup. Cut edges up so that ...

SOUTHERN FEATHER ROLLS

These rolls come from the southern United States, where dinner rolls as light as a feather are the pride of many a table.

MAKES 12	INGREDIENTS	MAKES 18
1	egg	2
2 tbsp	water	3 tbsp
¾ cup	milk	1 cup
3 tbsp	butter	4½ tbsp
2 tbsp	sugar	3 tbsp
1 tsp	salt	1½ tsp
2 cups	bread flour	3 cups
1½ tsp	yeast	2¼ tsp

METHOD

Put ingredients in bread pan in order suggested by your bread machine instructions. Set for dough stage. Press Start.

Butter muffin tins: 12 cups for the smaller recipe, 18 cups for the larger recipe.

When dough is ready, flour your hands. Remove dough from bread pan and place on floured surface. This dough is very soft and sticky. If your bread machine has not punched it down, knead dough lightly, just enough to press out air but incorporate as little additional flour as possible. Keeping your hands lightly floured, shape the dough into a fat log and cut into 12 equal pieces for the smaller recipe, 18 pieces for the larger.

Place each piece into a muffin cup. Put rolls in a warm place to rise for 40 minutes. Bake in a preheated 350°F oven until tops are just lightly browned, 20 to 25 minutes.

WHOLE-WHEAT SESAME ROLLS

These rolls are basic whole-wheat rolls, made from a slightly stiff dough so the rounds hold their shape on the baking sheet.

MAKES 8	INGREDIENTS	MAKES 12
⅔ cup	water	1 cup
1 tbsp	vegetable oil	1½ tbsp
1 tbsp	sugar	1½ tbsp
1 tsp	salt	1½ tsp
1 cup	bread flour	1½ cups
1 cup	whole-wheat flour	1½ cups
1½ tsp	yeast	2¼ tsp

TOPPING

2–3 tbsp milk
2–3 tbsp sesame seeds

METHOD

Put all dough ingredients in bread pan in order suggested by your bread machine instructions. Set for dough. Press Start.

When dough is ready, punch it down on a lightly floured board. Let it rest a few minutes, then take it between your hands and roll it into a thick log. Cut log into 8 equal pieces for the smaller recipe, 12 pieces for the larger recipe. Roll each piece into a ball, flatten slightly and put on one or two nonstick or lightly buttered baking sheets. Cover, put in a warm place and let rise for 1 hour.

When dough has risen, brush lightly with milk and sprinkle with sesame seeds. Cut a cross in the top of each. Bake in a preheated 375°F oven until light brown, 15 to 18 minutes.

RIGHT Whole-wheat Sesame Rolls

RYE CRESCENT ROLLS

These rye dinner rolls add an elegant touch to any meal, casual or formal. They're so good that they don't need butter.

MAKES 16	INGREDIENTS	MAKES 24
⅔ cup	flat beer	1 cup
2 tbsp	vegetable oil	3 tbsp
1 tbsp	honey	1½ tbsp
1 tsp	salt	1½ tsp
1 tsp	caraway seeds	1½ tsp
1½ cups	bread flour	2¼ cups
¾ cup	rye flour	1⅛ cups
2 tsp	yeast	1 tbsp
2 tbsp	melted butter	3 tbsp

METHOD

Put all ingredients except melted butter in bread pan in order suggested by your bread machine instructions. Set for whole-wheat bread, dough stage. Press Start.

When dough is ready, remove it from the bread machine and punch it down. Cut the smaller recipe into two equal parts, the larger recipe into three parts. Let the dough rest for five minutes. Oil two or three baking sheets.

On a lightly floured surface, roll out the first section of dough into a circle 8 to 9 inches in diameter. Cut the circle into eight wedges. Starting from the outside of the circle and working toward the point, loosely roll up each wedge. Stretch each roll slightly and pull it into a curve. Set it on the baking sheet with the point underneath. Repeat with all the wedges, then with the remaining dough.

Let the dough rise until doubled, about 1 hour. Brush rolls with melted butter. Bake in a preheated 400°F oven until rolls are lightly browned, 12 to 15 minutes.

SEMOLINA BREAD

Semolina is a hard winter wheat or durum flour used to make pasta, but it also makes a good bread when mixed with other flours. By itself, it makes a very heavy, dense bread. However, this loaf, great with pasta, is light and flavorful.

1 lb LOAF	INGREDIENTS	1½ lb LOAF
¾ cup	water	1⅛ cups
1 tsp	sugar	1½ tsp
1 tsp	salt	1½ tsp
1½ cups	bread flour	2¼ cups
⅔ cup	semolina flour	1 cup
1½ tsp	yeast	2¼ tsp

GLAZE

1 egg yolk beaten with 1 tsp water

2–3 tbsp sesame seeds

METHOD

Put all dough ingredients in bread machine pan. Set for white bread, dough stage. Press Start.

When dough is ready, remove from pan and punch down. Shape it into a fat baguette. Set it on a baking sheet that has been sprinkled with cornmeal. Cover dough and put in a warm place to rise until doubled, about 45 minutes.

Brush loaf with egg glaze and sprinkle with sesame seeds. Bake bread in preheated 375°F oven until golden and bread sounds hollow when rapped on the bottom, about 30 minutes.

PESTO SWIRL BREAD

A delicious layer of pesto is spread on a light whole-wheat dough, rolled up and baked into a tasty loaf that goes well with soups, salads, pastas, and grilled meat and fish. You can use store-bought pesto or make your own, following the recipe below. It's important that you drain off excess oil from the pesto, but it can be added to the bread instead of plain oil.

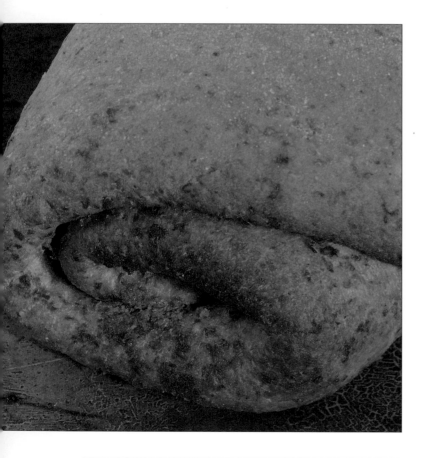

1 lb LOAF	INGREDIENTS	1½ lb LOAF
½ cup	water	¾ cup
¼ cup	milk	6 tbsp
1 tbsp	vegetable oil	1½ tbsp
1 tbsp	sugar	1½ tbsp
1 tsp	salt	1½ tsp
1½ cups	bread flour	2¼ cups
½ cup	whole-wheat flour	¾ cup
2 tsp	yeast	1 tbsp
¼ cup	pesto	6 tbsp

METHOD

Put all ingredients except pesto in bread pan in order suggested by your bread machine instructions. Set for whole-wheat bread, dough stage. Press Start.

Butter a 9½-inch loaf pan (large enough for either recipe).

Remove dough from bread machine and punch down. Let it rest 5 minutes. Roll it out on a lightly floured surface to form a rectangle about 8 inches wide and 14 to 18 inches long. Spread pesto evenly over surface. Roll the dough into a fat 8-inch cylinder. Tucking the edge under, put it in the loaf pan. Loosely cover and put in a warm place to rise for 1 hour.

Bake the loaf in a preheated 350°F oven until top is golden and a skewer inserted in the bread comes out clean, 30 to 35 minutes. Remove the bread from the pan and put it on a wire rack to cool for at least 15 minutes.

PESTO

INGREDIENTS

1 cup fresh
basil leaves

2 tbsp walnut pieces

1 clove garlic, peeled

¼ cup Parmesan
cheese

pinch salt

about 2 tbsp olive oil

METHOD

Put all ingredients except olive oil in blender. Blend, adding a little oil at a time. Keep the pesto rough and fairly dry so that oil doesn't soak into the dough.

WHOLE-WHEAT POTATO CLOVERLEAF ROLLS

These light whole-wheat rolls are excellent with dinner. If desired, add ½ tsp dried oregano or dill, or 2 tsp fresh snipped chives.

MAKES 12-16	INGREDIENTS	MAKES 18-24
½ cup	mashed potatoes	¼ cup
1	egg	1
¼ cup	milk	½ cup
1 tbsp	vegetable oil	1½ tbsp
1 tbsp	sugar	1½ tbsp
1 tsp	salt	1½ tsp
1⅓ cups	bread flour	2 cups
⅔ cup	whole-wheat flour	1 cup
2 tsp	yeast	1 tbsp
about 3 tbsp	melted butter	about 4 tbsp

METHOD

Put all ingredients except melted butter in bread pan in order suggested by your bread machine instructions. Set for whole-wheat bread, dough stage. Press Start.

Lightly oil 12 to 16 muffin cups for the smaller recipe, 18 to 24 muffin cups for the larger recipe.

When dough is ready, remove from bread machine and punch down. Cut smaller recipe into 12 to 16 equal pieces, the larger recipe into 18 to 24 pieces. Cut each piece into thirds. Roll each piece into a tiny ball and dip in the melted butter. Place three tiny balls in each muffin cup. Cover loosely and set in a warm place to rise until doubled, 45 minutes to 1 hour.

Preheat oven to 375°F. Lightly brush tops of rolls with remaining melted butter. Bake 15 to 20 minutes, until tops are golden brown.

Pumpernickel Raisin Rolls

Soft and slightly sweet pumpernickel raisin rolls are delicious with dinner.

MAKES 8-12	INGREDIENTS	MAKES 12-16
1	egg	1
½ cup	milk	⅞ cup
3 tbsp	vegetable oil	4½ tbsp
2 tbsp	molasses	3 tbsp
½ tsp	salt	¾ tsp
2 tbsp	unsweetened cocoa powder	3 tbsp
1 tsp	caraway seeds	1½ tsp
¾ cup	bread flour	1¼ cups
¾ cup	whole-wheat flour	1¼ cups
¾ cup	rye flour	1¼ cups
2 tsp	yeast	1 tbsp
3 tbsp	raisins	4½ tbsp
1 tbsp	melted butter	1½ tbsp

METHOD

Put all ingredients except raisins in bread pan in order suggested by your bread machine instructions. Set for whole-wheat bread, dough stage. Press Start. Add the raisins after the first kneading or when the machine signals it's time to add fruit.

Lightly oil an 8- or 9-inch square pan for the smaller recipe, a 9 × 13-inch pan for the larger recipe.

When dough is ready, remove from bread machine and punch down. Cut smaller recipe into 8 to 12 equal pieces, the larger recipe into 12 to 16 pieces. Roll each piece into a ball – they do not have to be perfectly round. Place balls about ½ inch apart in baking pan. Cover loosely and set in a warm place to rise until doubled, about 1 hour.

Preheat oven to 400°F. Lightly brush tops of rolls with melted butter. Bake 12 to 15 minutes, until a skewer inserted in roll comes out clean.

French Bread

This recipe produces wonderful baguettes when still warm, but they become stale within a day.

1 lb LOAF	INGREDIENTS	1½ lb LOAF
¾ cup	water	1 cup
1 tsp	salt	1½ tsp
2 cups	bread flour	3 cups
2 tsp	yeast	1 tbsp

METHOD

Put ingredients in bread pan in order suggested by your bread machine instructions. Set for French bread, medium crust.

To make baguettes, remove dough from bread machine after first kneading and punch down. Cut into two equal pieces. On a lightly floured surface, roll each piece into a thick rope, about 8 inches long for the 1-pound loaf, and 10 inches for the larger loaf. Place on a baking sheet that has been sprinkled with cornmeal. With a sharp knife, cut several diagonal slashes in the top of each loaf. Put dough in a warm place, cover loosely, and let rise until doubled in volume, 45 minutes to 1 hour. Make a wash of 1 tbsp egg white plus 1 tbsp water. Lightly brush wash over surface of loaves. Bake baguettes in preheated 400°F oven for about 25 minutes, until crust is golden brown and bread makes a hollow sound when thumped on the bottom and the top.

For crustier bread, place a shallow pan of boiling water on the bottom shelf of the oven. Or lightly spray water from a spray bottle into the oven when baking begins, and one or two more times during baking.

RIGHT Pumpernickel Raisin Rolls

GARLIC PEPPER POTATO ROLLS

These light dinner rolls are seasoned with garlic and black pepper, and will complement almost any entrée.

MAKES 8-12	INGREDIENTS	MAKES 12-16
1	egg	1 + 1 yolk
3 tbsp	milk	4½ tbsp
½ cup	mashed potatoes	¾ cup
2 tbsp	vegetable oil	3 tbsp
1 tbsp	sugar	1½ tbsp
2	cloves garlic, minced	3
1½ tsp	fresh-ground black pepper	2¼ tsp
1 tsp	salt	1½ tsp
2 cups	bread flour	3 cups
1½ tsp	yeast	2¼ tsp
2 tbsp	milk	3 tbsp

METHOD

Put all ingredients except milk in bread pan in order suggested by your bread machine instructions. Set for white bread, dough stage. Press Start.

Lightly oil an 8- or 9-inch square pan for the smaller recipe, a 9 × 13-inch pan for the larger recipe.

When dough is ready, remove from bread machine and punch down. Cut smaller recipe into 8 to 12 equal pieces, the larger recipe into 12 to 16 pieces. Roll each piece into a ball – it does not have to be perfectly round. Place balls about ½ inch apart in baking pan. Cover loosely and set in a warm place to rise until doubled, 45 minutes to 1 hour.

Preheat oven to 375°F. Lightly brush tops of rolls with milk. Bake 12 to 15 minutes, until rolls are golden and a skewer inserted in roll comes out clean.

ENGLISH MUFFINS

These English muffins are a bit crisper than the soft, store-bought kind, but they have a fresher flavor. The easiest way to make them is with a 3-inch round cookie cutter and a griddle, but you can use a clean tuna or pineapple can and a large skillet.

MAKES 10-12	INGREDIENTS	MAKES 15-18
¼ cup	water	6 tbsp
½ tbsp	baking soda	¼ tsp
½ cup	milk	¾ cup
2 tbsp	vegetable oil	3 tbsp
2 tsp	sugar	1 tbsp
½ tsp	salt	¾ tsp
2 cups	bread flour	3 cups
2 tsp	yeast	1 tbsp
	cornmeal	

METHOD

Dissolve the baking soda in the water. Put the water and remaining ingredients except cornmeal in bread pan in order suggested by your bread machine instructions. Set for white bread, dough stage. Press Start.

Sprinkle cornmeal on a baking sheet or large platter. White cornmeal is more esthetically pleasing on English muffins, but yellow will do the job just fine. When dough is ready, remove it and punch it down and cut it in half. Let it rest 5 minutes. Then on a lightly floured surface, roll out the first half to ⅜ inch thick. With the cookie cutter, cut out 3-inch rounds. Put the rounds on the cornmeal-covered baking sheet, then turn to coat both sides. Repeat with the second half. If you wish, you may roll up the scraps, knead them a little, let the dough rest a few minutes, then roll it out and cut a few more muffins. Don't reroll yet again – the muffins will be tough.

Cover muffins and let them rise 45 minutes.

If you have a griddle, set it for moderate heat. If not, place a skillet – preferably one with a non-stick finish – over moderate heat. If the griddle or pan is well-seasoned, it will not require oil. If not, use just the barest trace of oil to cook. Cook until muffin bottoms are nicely browned, then turn and cook the other side. Cooking time will vary from 6 to 10 minutes per side according to the temperature of your stove.

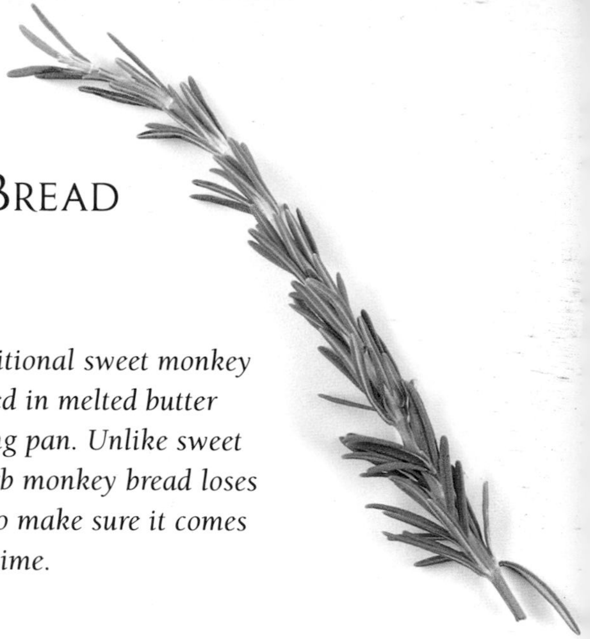

GARLIC HERB MONKEY BREAD

This savory pull-apart bread is a variation on the traditional sweet monkey bread. Small balls of garlic-flavored dough are dipped in melted butter seasoned with garlic and herbs, and layered in a baking pan. Unlike sweet monkey bread, which tastes good hot or cold, garlic-herb monkey bread loses its charm when cold, so time the making of the bread to make sure it comes out of the oven 5 minutes before meal time.

1 lb LOAF	INGREDIENTS	1½ lb LOAF
¾ cup	milk	1½ cups
2 tbsp	vegetable oil	3 tbsp
1 tsp	sugar	1½ tsp
1 tsp	salt	1½ tsp
1	clove garlic, pressed	1 or 2 small
1½ cups	bread flour	2¼ cups
½ cup	whole-wheat flour	¾ cup
1½ tsp	yeast	2¼ tsp
4 tbsp	butter	6 tbsp
2	cloves garlic, pressed	3
¼ tsp	dried sage	¼ tsp
¼ tsp	dried rosemary, crushed	¼ tsp
½ tsp	dried basil	¾ tsp

METHOD

Put first eight ingredients in bread pan in order suggested by your bread machine instructions. Set for whole-wheat bread, dough stage. Press Start.

A few minutes before dough is ready, melt butter in small skillet. Add garlic and herbs. Sauté for 2 minutes. If the garlic or herbs brown too quickly, remove the pan from the heat and let the mixture continue cooking in its own heat. The garlic will give the bread a bitter flavor if it burns. Lightly oil baking dish.

Remove the dough from the bread machine and punch down. Roll dough into a thick log and cut out into 20 to 24 pieces for the small loaf, 30 to 36 pieces for the large loaf. Roll pieces of dough into balls (they do not need to be perfectly round). Dip each ball in butter-herb mixture and layer in baking pan. The pieces in the first layer should be close but not touching to give them room to rise. On each succeeding layer, place balls so they overlap empty spaces on the layer beneath. Drizzle any remaining butter over the dough in the pan.

Cover dough loosely and put it in a warm place to rise. When bread has doubled in volume, about 30 to 40 minutes, put it in preheated 350°F oven. Bake until bread is lightly browned and a skewer inserted comes out clean, about 25 to 30 minutes. Invert bread on serving plate, remove baking pan, and serve.

If you need more time to coincide the baking with serving a meal, you can slow down the rising by putting the assembled bread in the refrigerator, then letting it return to room temperature before baking. Monkey bread is traditionally baked in a tube pan, 10 inches across for the larger loaf, a 7- or 8-inch pan for the smaller loaf. However, it looks impressive and tastes just as good when baked in round casserole dishes, about 1 inch smaller in diameter than the tube pan.

FOCCACIO WITH OLIVES AND SUN-DRIED TOMATOES

This foccacio is full of flavor and is best served plain. It should be eaten hot from the oven.

1lb LOAF	INGREDIENTS	1½lb LOAF
⅔ cup	water	1 cup
2 tbsp	olive oil	3 tbsp
1 tsp	salt	1½ tsp
¼ tsp	dried thyme	½ tsp
½ tsp	dried oregano	¾ tsp
2 cups	bread flour	3 cups
1¼ tsp	yeast	2 tsp
¼ cup	chopped sun-dried tomatoes	6 tbsp
¼ cup	kalamata olives, coarsely chopped	6 tbsp
2 tbsp	olive oil	3 tbsp
¼ cup	grated Asiago cheese	6 tbsp

METHOD

Put first seven ingredients in bread pan in order suggested by your bread machine instructions. Set for dough stage. Press Start. After about 15 minutes or when the beeper signals time to add fruit, add tomatoes and olives.

When dough is ready, punch it down on a lightly floured board. Let it rest a few minutes, then roll it into a round about ½ inch thick. Sprinkle cornmeal on a baking sheet. Put the dough on the baking sheet. Spread remaining olive oil over the top and sprinkle with the cheese. Bake bread in a preheated 400°F oven until lightly browned, about 20 minutes.

Cilantro Pesto Bread

A spicy filling of cilantro pesto with ricotta cheese and jalapeño chile gives this egg bread a deliciously different character. It goes well with grilled meat or spicy soup and is also good on its own.

1lb LOAF	INGREDIENTS	1½lb LOAF
½ cup	milk	⅔ cup
1	egg	2
2 tbsp	butter	3 tbsp
1 tbsp	sugar	1½ tbsp
1 small	jalapeño chile, chopped fine	1 large
1 tsp	salt	1½ tsp
2 cups	bread flour	3 cups
1½ tsp	yeast	2¼ tsp

FILLING

1lb LOAF		1½lb LOAF
⅓ cup	ricotta cheese	½ cup
¼ cup	fresh cilantro, tightly packed	6 tbsp
1	clove garlic, chopped	1½ cloves
2 tbsp	chopped walnuts	3 tbsp
½ small	jalapeño chile, chopped	1 small
1 tsp	olive oil	1½ tsp
½ tsp	salt	¾ tsp
¼ tsp	fresh-ground black pepper	½ tsp

METHOD

Put dough ingredients in bread pan in order suggested by your bread machine instructions. Set for white bread, dough stage. Press Start.

While the dough is working, make the filling. Start immediately as the ricotta must have time to drain completely. Put the ricotta in a colander to let it drain, at least 30 minutes. Stir once or twice to release liquids.

While ricotta is draining, put the remaining filling ingredients in a food processor or blender and process until a coarse paste forms. Do not allow the paste to become too smooth. When the ricotta is thoroughly drained, stir in the pesto.

When dough is ready, punch it down on a lightly floured board. Let it rest a few minutes. Butter a 9½-inch loaf pan (can be smaller for smaller loaf). Roll the dough out into a rectangle no wider than the length of the bread pan. Gently spread the filling over the surface of the bread, taking care not to tear the dough. Starting at the short end, roll dough into a cylinder. If necessary, turn ends under. Put the dough into the bread pan, seam side down. Cover and let rise in a warm place for 1 hour.

Bake in a preheated 350°F oven until golden, about 35 to 40 minutes.

TIP

TUSCAN SAGE WHOLE-WHEAT BREAD

Flavored with fresh sage that has been sautéed in olive oil, this bread is delicious with game or roast meats.

1lb LOAF	INGREDIENTS	1½lb LOAF
12 leaves	fresh sage	18 leaves
2 tbsp	olive oil	3 tbsp
⅔ cup	water	1 cup
1 tbsp	sugar	1½ tbsp
1 tsp	salt	1½ tsp
⅔ cup	whole-wheat flour	1 cup
1⅓ cups	bread flour	2 cups
2 tsp	yeast	1 tbsp

TOPPING

1 egg, lightly beaten with a fork
2 tsp water
freshly cracked pepper

METHOD

Tear sage leaves into several pieces. Heat oil in small skillet. Add sage to oil and sauté for 1 minute, removing from heat sooner if oil is too hot. Leaves must not be scorched. Let cool for 10 minutes. Put sage, oil, and remaining dough ingredients in bread pan in order suggested by your bread machine instructions. Set for whole-wheat bread, dough stage. Press Start.

When dough is ready, punch it down on a lightly floured board. Let it rest a few minutes. Sprinkle cornmeal on a baking sheet. Shape the dough into a round and put it on the baking sheet. Combine the egg and water and brush over the top of the dough. Sprinkle cracked pepper over top. Cover and let rise in a warm place for 1 hour.

With a sharp knife, make three slashes in the top of the bread. Place in a preheated 375°F oven and bake until the top is golden brown, 30 to 45 minutes.

SPINACH CHEESE SWIRL

A tender, flavorful whole-wheat dough is wrapped around a savory filling of ricotta cheese, spinach, onions, and thyme. Try this with meatloaf sandwiches or as a hearty accompaniment to soup or salad.

1lb LOAF	INGREDIENTS	1½lb LOAF
½ cup	mashed potatoes	¾ cup
½ cup	milk	¾ cup
2 tbsp	butter	3 tbsp
1 tbsp	sugar	1½ tbsp
½ tsp	dried thyme	¾ tsp
1 tsp	salt	1½ tsp
1⅓ cups	bread flour	2 cups
⅔ cup	whole-wheat flour	1 cup
1½ tsp	yeast	2¼ tsp

FILLING

1lb LOAF	INGREDIENTS	1½lb LOAF
⅓ cup	ricotta cheese	½ cup
⅓ cup	chopped cooked spinach	½ cup
1 tsp	olive oil	1½ tsp
3 tbsp	chopped onion	4½ tbsp
½ tsp	salt	¾ tsp
¼ tsp	pepper	½ tsp
¼ tsp	dried thyme	½ tsp

METHOD

Put dough ingredients in bread pan in order suggested by your bread machine instructions. Set for whole-wheat bread, dough stage. Press Start.

When dough is working, make the filling. Start immediately, because the spinach and ricotta must have time to drain completely. Put the spinach and ricotta in separate colanders to let them drain, at least 30 minutes. Stir once or twice to release liquids. Squeeze the spinach by hand to remove additional water and press between a double thickness of paper towels.

Heat the olive oil in a small skillet and sauté the onions for 5 minutes. Remove from heat and let cool slightly. Then combine the spinach, cheese, onion and seasonings.

When dough is ready, punch it down on a lightly floured board. Let it rest a few minutes. Butter a 9½-inch loaf pan (can be smaller for smaller loaf). Roll the dough out into a rectangle no wider than the length of the bread pan. Gently spread the spinach-cheese filling over the surface of the bread, taking care not to tear the dough. Starting at the short end, roll dough into a cylinder. Put the dough into the bread pan, seam side down. Cover and let rise in a warm place for 1 hour.

Bake in a preheated 350°F oven until golden, about 35 to 40 minutes.

NOTE

This recipe is based on pure mashed potatoes with no additions. If milk or other liquids have been added to the potatoes, check during kneading and add a little flour if dough is too wet.

WHOLE-WHEAT PESTO FOCCACIO

This simple flatbread should be eaten warm. It can be served plain or dipped in a high-quality extra-virgin olive oil.

1lb LOAF	INGREDIENTS	1½lb LOAF
⅔ cup	water	1 cup
2 tbsp	olive oil	3 tbsp
1 tsp	salt	1½ tsp
1 cup	bread flour	1½ cups
1 cup	whole-wheat flour	1½ cups
1¼ tsp	yeast	2 tsp
¼ cup	prepared pesto	6 tbsp
2 tbsp	pine nuts or chopped walnuts	3 tbsp

METHOD

Put all but the last two ingredients in bread pan in order suggested by your bread machine instructions. Set for whole-wheat dough. Press Start.

When dough is ready, punch it down on a lightly floured board. Let it rest a few minutes, then roll it into a round about ½ inch thick. Sprinkle cornmeal on a baking sheet. Put the dough on the baking sheet. Spread the pesto over the top and sprinkle nuts over pesto. Bake bread in a preheated 400°F oven until lightly browned, about 20 minutes.

7

SOURDOUGH BREADS

SOURDOUGH STARTER

Sourdough is often associated with the crusty, dense loaves for which San Francisco is famous, but its use in baking can be traced back to ancient Egypt, when much effort was made to disguise the sour taste. Sourdough is the product of fermentation in dough that has sat open to the air in warm temperatures for several days, gathering wild yeasts from the air.
Theoretically, a bread made with a good sourdough starter will not need any additional yeast as leavening, but such breads are often too dense and unleavened to suit most people's tastes. Today, sourdough starter is added to bread not for leavening, but to give it that sour taste that bakers once tried to disguise.
Making and maintaining your own pot of sourdough starter is not difficult, especially if you bake frequently. The first batch takes several days to develop a good sour taste, but after that it can be used and replenished daily.

INGREDIENTS

1 cup low-fat milk, scalded
1 cup hot water
1 tbsp sugar
2¼ tsp active dry yeast
2½ cups all-purpose or bread flour

METHOD

Mix the milk, hot water and sugar. Let cool to between 105°F and 115°F, then add the yeast. Let sit until the mixture develops a foamy head, about 5 to 10 minutes. Then add the flour and mix well.

Loosely cover the bowl with a lid that is partly ajar and put it in a warm place, between 80°F and 100°F. Leaving the bowl partly uncovered allows air to circulate and airborne yeasts to collect in the starter. Within 24 hours, it should be bubbly and develop a hint of a sour smell. Stir it once or twice a day. The mixture may separate, with a thick, gluey mixture at the bottom and a watery liquid floating on top. That's normal; just stir them together. The starter is ready to use when it develops a good sour smell, usually three to five days.

To bake sourdough bread, you need to prepare a "sponge" at least six hours in advance. Mix some starter with a portion of flour and liquid, as directed by the

recipe. Replenish the starter with amounts of flour and water equal to the amount you removed. For instance, if the recipe calls for ½ cup of sourdough starter, replenish the starter with ½ cup water and ½ cup flour. Both the sponge and the replenished starter should be put in a warm place, covered loosely, and left to ferment at least 6 hours, until bubbly.

If you use the starter frequently, more or less daily, you can leave it in its warm place all the time, replenishing it after each use. If you use it only occasionally, replenish it, let it sit out 24 hours, then cover tightly and refrigerate. If you don't bake at least weekly, refresh the starter every week or so. Remove 1 cup of the starter and discard the rest. Add 1 cup each of flour and water, let it sit out for 24 hours, then refrigerate.

NOTES

Every six months or so, add a pinch of sugar and yeast to the starter.

The starter will never look attractive; gray is its normal color. However, if the starter or the liquid develops a green or a pink cast, throw the whole thing out and start over.

SOURDOUGH BREAD

Sourdough can be stubborn and temperamental, and the bread it makes can vary with each baking. Because the starter is left open to collect wild yeasts from the air, one sourdough loaf can taste different from the next. In addition, the dough may require varying amounts of liquid because the starter also absorbs varying amounts of liquid from the air. Be patient, watch the dough as the bread machine kneads it and add a splash of water or a tablespoon of flour if it is needed. A traditional French sourdough loaf is made without sugar or fat. We have included a small amount of each – sugar to encourage the yeast to ferment, and butter so that the bread does not turn stale and hard too quickly. Purists can omit both.

INGREDIENTS

1lb LOAF		1½lb LOAF
SOURDOUGH SPONGE		
⅓ cup	sourdough starter	½ cup
¼ cup	water	6 tbsp
⅔ cup	bread flour	1 cup
BREAD		
5 tbsp	water	7½ tbsp
2 tsp	sugar	1 tbsp
1 tbsp	butter	1½ tbsp
1⅓ cups	bread flour	2 cups
1 tsp	salt	1½ tsp
1½ tsp	yeast	2¼ tsp

EGGWASH (OPTIONAL)

1 egg, beaten with a fork
2 tsp water

METHOD

At least 12 hours before baking, make the sourdough sponge by combining the sourdough starter, water, and flour. Stir and leave in a warm place overnight.

When you are ready to bake, put the sourdough sponge and all the bread ingredients in bread pan in order suggested by your bread machine instructions. Set for dough. Press Start. You may need to adjust liquid or flour slightly, depending on the water content of your sourdough starter.

When dough is ready, punch it down on a lightly floured board. Let it rest a few minutes. Sprinkle cornmeal on a baking sheet. Shape the dough into a round and put it on the baking sheet. Cover and let rise in a warm place for 1 hour.

Combine the egg and water, if using, and brush over the top of the dough. With a sharp knife, make three slashes in the top of the bread. Place in a preheated 375°F oven and bake until the top is golden brown, 30 to 50 minutes.

SOURDOUGH RYE RAISIN BREAD

This is a chewy sourdough with good flavor and a hint of sweetness added by the molasses and raisins.

1lb LOAF	INGREDIENTS	1½lb LOAF
	SOURDOUGH SPONGE	
⅓ cup	sourdough starter	½ cup
¼ cup	water	6 tbsp
⅔ cup	rye flour	1 cup
	BREAD	
¼ cup	water	6 tbsp
1 tbsp	butter	1½ tbsp
2 tbsp	molasses	3 tbsp
1 tbsp	unsweetened cocoa	1½ tbsp
1 tsp	salt	1½ tsp
1⅓ cups	bread flour	2 cups
1½ tsp	yeast	2¼ tsp
⅓ cup	raisins	½ cup

EGG WASH

1 egg, beaten with a fork
2 tsp water

METHOD

At least 12 hours before baking, make the sourdough sponge by combining the sourdough starter, water, and rye flour. Stir and leave in a warm place overnight.

Put sourdough sponge in bread pan along with all the bread ingredients except the raisins in the order suggested by your bread machine instructions. Set for dough. Press Start. You may need to adjust liquid or flour slightly, depending on the water content of your sourdough starter. After 15 minutes or when beeper sounds to add fruit, add raisins.

When dough is ready, punch it down on a lightly floured board. Let it rest a few minutes. Sprinkle cornmeal on a baking sheet. Shape the dough into a round and put it on the baking sheet. Cover, put in a warm place and let rise until doubled in bulk, to about 60 minutes. Combine the egg and water and brush over the top. With a sharp knife, make three slashes in the top of the bread. Place in a preheated 375°F oven and bake for about 30 to 45 minutes, until golden brown.

SOURDOUGH BREAD WITH ROASTED GARLIC AND PEPPERS

Roasted sweet red peppers are the dominant flavor here, backed up by thyme and a subtle taste of garlic.

1lb LOAF	INGREDIENTS	1½lb LOAF
	SOURDOUGH SPONGE	
⅓ cup	sourdough starter	½ cup
¼ cup	water	6 tbsp
⅔ cup	bread flour	1 cup
	BREAD	
1 small	whole garlic head	1 large
1 tbsp	olive oil	1 tbsp
⅓ cup	chopped roasted red pepper	½ cup
3 tbsp	water	4½ tbsp
2 tsp	sugar	1 tbsp
1 tsp	salt	1½ tsp
1⅓ cups	bread flour	2 cups
1½ tsp	yeast	2¼ tsp

METHOD

At least 12 hours before baking, make the sourdough sponge by combining the sourdough starter, water, and flour. Stir and leave in a warm place overnight.

To roast the garlic, remove the outer papery husks. Put on a doubled piece of aluminum foil, pour olive oil over top of garlic and turn so all surfaces are oiled. Wrap the foil around the garlic so it is completely enclosed. Bake in a 350°F oven for about 40 minutes, until cloves are soft like butter. Remove from oven and let cool, then cut open each clove and squeeze out the garlic.

To roast red pepper, cut about half a pepper into several fairly flat pieces. Put on a broiler pan or a flat piece of aluminum foil, skin side up. Place under the broiler and cook until skin is blackened and blistered. Remove and put immediately in a paper bag or a covered dish so pepper can steam as it cools. This loosens the skin. When pepper is cool enough to handle, peel off and discard skin – it's OK if a few bits remain – and dice pepper.

Put sourdough sponge, garlic and remaining ingredients except peppers in bread pan in order suggested by your bread machine instructions. Set for white bread, dough stage. Press Start. After about 15 minutes or when the beeper signals time to add fruit, add diced pepper.

When dough is ready, punch it down on a lightly floured board. Let it rest a few minutes. Sprinkle cornmeal on a baking sheet. Shape the dough into a round and put it on the baking sheet. Cover and let rise in a warm place for 1 hour.

With a sharp knife, make three slashes in the top of the bread, then make three more slashes at a diagonal. Place

SOURDOUGH ROSEMARY BREAD WITH OLIVES

This is a tantalizing sourdough bread, fragrant with rosemary and studded with bits of olive. It is best served warm with sweet butter but is also delicious with strong cheeses.

1lb LOAF	INGREDIENTS	1½lb LOAF
	SOURDOUGH SPONGE	
⅓ cup	sourdough starter	½ cup
¼ cup	water	6 tbsp
⅔ cup	bread flour	1 cup
	BREAD	
1 tsp	chopped fresh rosemary	1½ tsp
2 tbsp	olive oil	3 tbsp
5 tbsp	water	7½ tbsp
1⅓ cups	bread flour	2 cups
1 tsp	salt	1½ tsp
1½ tsp	yeast	2¼ tsp
¼ cup	coarsely chopped kalamata olives	6 tbsp

EGGWASH

1 egg, beaten with a fork

2 tsp water

METHOD

At least 12 hours before baking, make the sourdough sponge by combining the sourdough starter, water, and flour. Stir and leave in a warm place overnight.

When you are ready to bake, put the rosemary in a small microwave-safe dish with the olive oil. Heat until the oil is hot and the rosemary barely starts to sizzle in the microwave, about 90 seconds on High. Let the rosemary steep in the oil at least 15 minutes, then strain and discard the rosemary. Save the oil for the bread. (You can also heat the oil on the stovetop in a small pan, add the rosemary and remove from the heat.)

Put the sourdough sponge, the rosemary oil, and all the bread ingredients except the olives in bread pan in order suggested by your bread machine instructions. Set for dough. Press Start. You may need to adjust liquid or flour slightly, depending on the water content of your sourdough starter. After about 15 minutes or when the beeper signals time to add fruit, add olives.

When dough is ready, punch it down on a lightly floured board. Let it rest a few minutes. Sprinkle cornmeal on a baking sheet. Shape the dough into a round and put it on the baking sheet. Cover and let rise in a warm place for 1 hour.

Combine the egg and water and brush over the top of the dough. With a sharp knife, make three slashes in the top of the bread. Place in a preheated 375°F oven and bake until the top is golden brown, 30 to 50 minutes.

Whole-wheat Sourdough Bread with Sun-dried Tomatoes

This crusty round of bread, flavored with sun-dried tomatoes, thyme, and cracked pepper, is delicious topped with cheese or in a meatloaf sandwich.

1lb LOAF	INGREDIENTS	1½lb LOAF
	SOURDOUGH SPONGE	
⅓ cup	sourdough starter	½ cup
¼ cup	water	6 tbsp
⅔ cup	whole-wheat flour	1 cup
	BREAD	
3 tbsp	water	4½ tbsp
1 tbsp	olive oil	1½ tbsp
1 tbsp	sugar	1½ tbsp
1 tsp	dried thyme	1½ tsp
1½ tsp	cracked black pepper	2¼ tsp
1 tsp	salt	1½ tsp
1⅓ cups	bread flour	2 cups
2 tsp	yeast	1 tbsp
¼ cup	chopped sun-dried tomatoes	6 tbsp

METHOD

At least 12 hours before baking, make the sourdough sponge by combining the sourdough starter, water, and whole-wheat flour. Stir and leave in a warm place overnight.

If tomatoes are stored in oil, blot dry. You can substitute the tomato oil for the olive oil, if you wish.

Put sourdough sponge and all other ingredients except tomatoes in bread pan in order suggested by your bread machine instructions. Set for whole-wheat bread, dough stage. Press Start. After about 15 minutes or when the beeper signals time to add fruit, add tomatoes.

When dough is ready, punch it down on a lightly floured board. Let it rest for a few minutes. Sprinkle cornmeal on a baking sheet. Shape the dough into a round and put it on the baking sheet. Cover and let rise in a warm place for 1 hour.

With a sharp knife, make three slashes in the top of the bread, then make three more slashes at a diagonal. Place in a preheated 375°F oven and bake until the top is golden brown, 30 to 45 minutes.

WHOLE-WHEAT SOURDOUGH WITH BULGUR

This sourdough bread, baked in the bread machine, gets its slightly coarse texture from the bulgur wheat. Perhaps more than other sourdough breads, the liquid content varies depending on the sourdough starter and how well the bulgur is drained, so the dough should be monitored during the kneading stage and liquid adjusted if needed.

1lb LOAF	INGREDIENTS	1½lb LOAF
	SOURDOUGH SPONGE	
⅓ cup	sourdough starter	½ cup
¼ cup	water	6 tbsp
⅔ cup	whole-wheat flour	1 cup
	BREAD	
¼ cup	bulgur	6 tbsp
2 cups	water	2 cups
about 4 tbsp	milk	about 6 tbsp
1 tbsp	butter	1½ tbsp
1 tbsp	sugar	1½ tbsp
1 tsp	salt	1½ tsp
1⅓ cups	bread flour	2 cups
2 tsp	yeast	1 tbsp

METHOD

At least 12 hours before baking, make the sourdough sponge by combining the sourdough starter, water, and whole-wheat flour. Stir and leave in a warm place overnight.

Just before starting the bread, put the bulgur wheat in a small pan with the water. Bring to a boil and let boil for 6 minutes. Remove from heat and drain. Let cool 15 minutes. Blot with paper towel to absorb any excess moisture.

Put sourdough sponge, bulgur and remaining ingredients in bread pan in order suggested by your bread machine instructions. Set for whole-wheat bread, medium crust. Press Start. Check consistency of dough

SOUTHWESTERN SPICED SOURDOUGH

This bread, which is also good when baked in the oven as a free-form loaf, is spiced with the traditional seasonings of the US Southwest – pure chile powder, ground cumin and oregano, preferably Mexican oregano. Use chile powder to suit your taste. I like it made with ancho chile powder, which is only moderately spicy. Take care if using hot New Mexico chile powder or cayenne. The spice labelled simply "chili powder" is not pure chile powder but a blend of chile and other spices. The bread is studded with pumpkin seeds, which are eaten like sunflower seeds. Called pepitas *in Spanish, shelled pumpkin seeds can be found in Mexican food stores and many supermarkets in the West and Southwest. If you use pumpkin seeds that are salted and roasted, reduce the salt in the recipe by ¼ teaspoon.*

1lb LOAF	INGREDIENTS	1½lb LOAF
	SOURDOUGH SPONGE	
⅓ cup	sourdough starter	½ cup
¼ cup	water	6 tbsp
⅔ cup	bread flour	1 cup
	BREAD	
3 tbsp	water	4½ tbsp
1 tbsp	butter	1½ tbsp
1 tbsp	sugar	1½ tbsp
1 tsp	salt	1½ tsp
1 tbsp	pure chile powder	1½ tbsp
½ tsp	ground cumin	¾ tsp
1 tsp	dried oregano	1½ tsp
1⅓ cups	bread flour	2 cups
1½ tsp	yeast	2¼ tsp
3 tbsp	shelled pumpkin seeds	4½ tbsp

TOPPING
(if baked in the oven)
1 egg
2 tsp water
shelled pumpkin seeds

METHOD

At least 12 hours before baking, make the sourdough sponge by combining the sourdough starter, water, and flour. Stir and leave in a warm place overnight.

Put sponge and all bread ingredients except pumpkin seeds in bread pan in order suggested by your bread machine instructions. Set for white bread, medium crust. Press Start. After about 15 minutes or when the beeper signals time to add fruit, add the pumpkin seeds.

To bake this bread in the oven, set the bread machine for dough stage. When it is ready, remove and punch down dough. Shape dough into a round and put on a baking sheet sprinkled with cornmeal.

Combine the egg and water and brush over the bread. Sprinkle some pumpkin seeds over the top.

Cover and let rise in a warm place until doubled in size, about 1 hour. With a sharp knife, make two parallel slashes in the top of the loaf. Bake in a preheated 375°F oven until brown, about 30 to 45 minutes.

SISTERON RYE BREAD

This is a sourdough adaptation of the round loaves of rye bread baked in the town of Sisteron, Provence. It is a dense bread, wonderful warm with sweet butter.

SOURDOUGH SPONGE

⅓ cup	sourdough starter	½ cup
¼ cup	water	6 tbsp
⅔ cup	pumpernickel flour	1 cup
2 tsp	caraway seeds	1 tbsp

BREAD

about ⅓ cup	water	about ½ cup
1 tsp	salt	1½ tsp
1⅓ cups	bread flour	2 cups
2 tsp	yeast	1 tbsp

TOPPING

1 egg
2 tsp water
caraway seeds, optional

METHOD

At least 12 hours before baking, make the sourdough sponge by combining the sourdough starter, water, pumpernickel flour, and caraway seeds. Stir and leave in a warm place overnight.

Put sourdough sponge and all the bread ingredients in bread pan in order suggested by your bread machine instructions. Set for dough. Press Start.

When dough is ready, punch it down on a lightly floured board. Let it rest a few minutes. Sprinkle cornmeal on a baking sheet. Shape the dough into a round and put it on the baking sheet. Cover and let rise in a warm place for 1 hour.

When dough has risen, combine the egg and water and brush over the top of the dough. With a sharp knife, cut a ring around the top of the dough. Sprinkle caraway seeds over top, if desired. Bake in a preheated 375°F oven until golden brown, 30 to 45 minutes.

SOURDOUGH RYE SEED BREAD

This crusty loaf is covered with a mix of five seeds – poppy, sesame, fennel, caraway, and flax – that give it unusual crunch and flavor, and a bakery-fresh appearance.

1lb LOAF	INGREDIENTS	1½lb LOAF
	SOURDOUGH SPONGE	
⅓ cup	sourdough starter	½ cup
¼ cup	water	6 tbsp
⅔ cup	rye flour	1 cup
	BREAD	
3 tbsp	water	4½ tbsp
1 tbsp	sugar	1½ tbsp
1 tsp	salt	1½ tsp
1⅓ cups	bread flour	2 cups
1½ tsp	yeast	2¼ tsp

TOPPINGS

1 egg, lightly beaten with 2 tsp water
For the 1-pound loaf: 2 teaspoons each fennel, caraway, poppy, sesame, and flax seeds
For the 1½-pound loaf: 1 tablespoon each fennel, caraway, poppy, sesame, and flax seeds

METHOD

At least 12 hours before baking, make the sourdough sponge by combining the sourdough starter, water, and flour. Stir and leave in a warm place overnight.

Put sourdough sponge and all the bread ingredients in bread pan in order suggested by your bread machine instructions. Set for whole-wheat bread, dough stage. Press Start.

When dough is ready, punch it down on a lightly floured board. Let it rest a few minutes. Then take it between your hands and roll it into a fat log, 10–12 inches long for the smaller loaf, 15–18 inches for the larger loaf. Brush with the egg wash.

Mix the seeds and spread them on a clean surface. Roll the top and sides of the bread in the seeds until loaf is thickly covered and all the seeds have been picked up. Put the bread on a baking sheet that has been sprinkled with cornmeal.

Cover and let rise 45 to 60 minutes. Bake in a preheated 375°F oven until top is golden and sounds hollow when thumped, about 30 to 45 minutes.

SOURDOUGH RYE BREAD

This rye bread makes great sandwiches. It can be baked in the bread machine, but is also good baked in the oven.

1 lb LOAF	INGREDIENTS	1½ lb LOAF
¼ cup	sourdough starter	6 tbsp
⅔ cup	water	1 cup
¾ cup	rye flour	1¼ cups
2 tsp	caraway seeds	1 tbsp
1 tbsp	vegetable oil	1½ tsp
1 tbsp	sugar	1½ tbsp
1 tsp	salt	1½ tsp
1⅔ cups	bread flour	2 cups
2 tsp	yeast	1 tbsp

METHOD

The night before baking bread, make a sponge by combining the sourdough starter, ⅓ cup water (½ cup for larger loaf), rye flour, and 1 tsp caraway seeds. Cover loosely and set in a warm place for at least 8 hours.

Put sponge and remaining ingredients in a bread pan in order suggested by your bread machine instructions. Set for whole-wheat bread, medium crust. Press Start.

To bake bread in a conventional oven, set the machine for the dough stage. Remove when dough is ready, punch down. Shape into a long, fat loaf or a round loaf. Place on a baking sheet slightly sprinkled with cornmeal. Cover loosely and put in a warm place to rise until doubled in volume, about 1 hour.

When bread has risen, make a wash of 1 lightly beaten egg and 1 tbsp water. Lightly brush the wash over the surface of the loaf, taking care not to deflate the dough. Bake bread in a preheated 350°F oven until bread is crusty and makes a hollow sound when tapped on the top and bottom.

SOURDOUGH WHOLE-WHEAT BREAD

This is a dense and flavorful bread, but it is not a high-riser.

1lb LOAF	INGREDIENTS	1½ lb LOAF
⅓ cup	sourdough starter	½ cup
⅓ cup	water	½ cup
¼ cup	cracked wheat	6 tbsp
2 tbsp	butter	3 tbsp
1 tbsp	honey	1½ tbsp
2 tbsp	dried milk	3 tbsp
1 tsp	salt	1½ tsp
1 cup	bread flour	1½ cups
1 cup	whole-wheat flour	1½ cups
1½ tsp	yeast	2¼ tsp

METHOD

The night before making bread, make the sponge by mixing sourdough starter, ½ cup bread flour, and about 2 tbsp water. Cover loosely and put in a warm place for at least 6 hours.

About 20 minutes before starting bread, put the cracked wheat in a small saucepan. Cover with water. Bring to a boil, then boil 6 minutes. Drain the wheat thoroughly, then let it cool at least 10 minutes.

Stir down the sponge and put it in the bread machine pan with the remainder of the water. Add cooled wheat and remaining ingredients in the order suggested by your bread machine instructions. Set for whole-wheat bread, medium crust. Press Start.

RIGHT Sourdough Whole-Wheat Bread

SOURDOUGH FRENCH BREAD

Sourdough bread can be both stubborn and temperamental, but it is also delicious. Unlike most of the other sourdough recipes in this book, the sourdough starter in this bread is a major ingredient, not just a small addition for extra flavor. The flavor will vary according to the type of sourdough starter you use and the airborne wild yeasts in your area. Because the sponge sits out for at least eight hours and absorbs moisture from the air, the amount of water you add may also vary.

1 lb LOAF	INGREDIENTS	1½ lb LOAF
⅔ cup	sourdough starter	1 cup
¼ cup	water	6 tbsp
2 tsp	sugar	1 tbsp
1 tsp	salt	1½ tsp
1¼ cups	bread flour	2⅓ cups
2 tsp	yeast	1 tbsp
1 tsp	cornstarch	1½ tsp
2 tbsp	water	3 tbsp

METHOD

The day before you bake the bread, make the sponge by mixing the starter, ¾ cup flour, and 2 tbsp water. Cover loosely and put in a warm place. Let sit at least 8 hours.

Put sponge, 2 tbsp water, sugar, salt, remaining flour, and yeast in bread pan in order suggested by your bread machine instructions. Set for French or white bread, dough stage. Press Start.

When dough is ready, remove from bread machine and punch down. Shape the dough into one short, fat loaf, one round loaf, or one baguette for the smaller recipe, two baguettes for the large one. Place loaf on baking sheet that has been sprinkled with cornmeal. Use a sharp knife to cut several diagonal slashes in the top. Cover bread loosely and set it in a warm place to rise. This is a slow-rising bread which may take an hour or longer.

Preheat oven to 400°F. When bread has risen, dissolve cornstarch in 2 tbsp water and lightly brush it over the surface of the bread. For crustier bread, place a shallow pan of boiling water on the bottom shelf of the oven, or use a spray bottle to squirt water into the oven several times while baking. Bake 35 to 40 minutes, until crust is browned and bread makes hollow sound on top and bottom when rapped with knuckles.

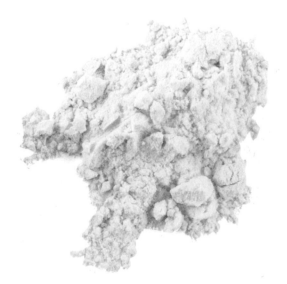

SOURDOUGH WALNUT RYE BREAD

This bread is good for meat or cheese sandwiches. Use walnut oil if you have it, otherwise substitute vegetable oil. Because the bread uses sourdough starter, the sponge should be made the night before baking.

1 lb LOAF	INGREDIENTS	1½ lb LOAF
½ cup	sourdough starter	¾ cup
7 tbsp	water	⅔ cup
1 tbsp	walnut or vegetable oil	1½ tbsp
1 tbsp	sugar	1½ tbsp
1 tsp	salt	1½ tsp
2 tbsp	cornmeal	3 tbsp
1 cup	rye flour	1½ cups
1 cup	bread flour	1½

METHOD

To make sponge, combine sourdough starter, ¼ cup of the water and ½ cup of the rye flour. Stir well. Cover it loosely and set it in a warm place to ferment overnight.

Put the sponge and all remaining ingredients except walnuts in bread pan in order suggested by your bread machine instructions. Set for whole-wheat bread, medium crust. Press Start. Add walnuts after the first

8

COFFEE CAKES AND SWEET BREADS

CINNAMON STICKY BUNS

These sweet, sticky buns can be assembled in advance and refrigerated overnight. In the morning, they will have to finish their second rising before you bake them.

MAKES 15	INGREDIENTS	MAKES 22
	DOUGH	
½ cup	milk	⅞ cup
1	egg	1
3 tbsp	butter	4½ tbsp
¼ cup	sugar	6 tbsp
½ tsp	salt	¾ tsp
2 cups	bread flour	3 cups
2 tsp	yeast	1 tbsp
	FILLING	
⅓ cup	brown sugar	½ cup
1 tsp	cinnamon	1½ tsp
2 tbsp	very soft butter	3 tbsp
	SYRUP	
3 tbsp	butter	4½ tbsp
½ cup	brown sugar	¾ cup
2 tbsp	water	3 tbsp
30	pecan halves	44

METHOD

Put dough ingredients in bread pan in order suggested by your bread machine instructions. Set for white or sweet bread, dough stage. Press Start.

Remove the dough from the bread machine and punch down. Let it rest for 5 minutes to make it easier to roll out. While dough is relaxing, mix brown sugar and cinnamon to make filling. For the smaller recipe, roll dough into a rectangle 7 to 8 inches wide and about 16 inches long. For the larger recipe, cut down in half and roll into two rectangles, each 7 to 8 inches wide and 11 to 12 inches long. Spread the soft butter over the surface of the dough. Thickly sprinkle brown sugar and cinnamon over the surface, spreading to edges. Roll dough into a long cylinder or cylinders. Slicing crosswise through the cylinder, cut into 15 pieces for the smaller recipe, 22 pieces for the larger.

The rolls can be baked together in baking pans or separately in muffin pans. The muffin-pan rolls are neater and crusty on the outside. If you cook them in baking pans, they will be softer. An 8-inch square baking pan is the perfect size for nine rolls; a 9 × 13-inch pan should hold 15 rolls.

Make the syrup by combining butter, brown sugar, and water in a small pan. Heat until butter is melted and sugar is dissolved. Stir well, then pour syrup into the bottoms of the baking pan or muffin-pan cups. Place two pecan halves in the bottom of each muffin cup, or on the top of each roll if you are using a baking pan. Place rolls in muffin cups, or turn them upside down (so pecans are on the bottom) in a baking pan. Cover rolls loosely, set them in a warm place, and let them rise until doubled, 45 minutes to 1 hour.

Bake rolls in a preheated 350°F oven until they are nicely browned, 17 to 22 minutes in a muffin pan, 20 to 25 minutes in a baking pan. The rolls must be removed from the pan immediately, or the sugar syrup will harden. Keeping in mind that excess sugar syrup will run off, invert the pan or muffin pan over a large plate or baking sheet. Let them cool slightly, or the hot sugar will burn your mouth.

Banana Nut Cinnamon Swirl

Banana is mixed into the dough of this breakfast bread. Before baking, the dough is rolled out, spread with butter, sprinkled with cinnamon, brown sugar, and pecans, and rolled up. When it's baked, it's similar to a not-overly sweet cinnamon roll.

1lb LOAF	INGREDIENTS	1½lb LOAF
1	egg	2
2 tbsp	milk	2 tbsp
⅓ cup	mashed ripe banana	½ cup
1 tbsp	butter	1½ tbsp
1 tbsp	sugar	1½ tbsp
1 tsp	salt	1½ tsp
2 cups	bread flour	3 cups
1½ tsp	yeast	2¼ tsp

	FILLING	
1 tbsp	very soft butter	1½ tbsp
2 tbsp	brown sugar	3 tbsp
½ tsp	cinnamon	¾ tsp
2 tbsp	chopped pecans	3 tbsp

METHOD

Put dough ingredients in bread pan in order suggested by your bread machine instructions. Set for white bread, dough stage. Press Start.

When dough is ready, punch it down on a lightly floured board. Let it rest a few minutes, then roll it out into an oval no more than 9 inches wide, or the length of your loaf pan. Spread the butter over the dough. Mix the brown sugar and cinnamon and sprinkle over the dough. Sprinkle the pecans over the sugar.

Roll the dough into a tight cylinder. Put the cylinder, down, into a buttered 9½-inch loaf pan (pan can be smaller for the smaller recipe). Rub some additional butter into the top of the loaf. Cover, put in a warm place and let rise for 1 hour.

When bread has risen, bake in a preheated 350°F oven until the top is golden brown, about 30 to 45 minutes.

RICH CALIFORNIA HONEY FIG BREAD

This is a sweet bread, flavored with figs, rum, vanilla, and honey. Because of the high sugar content, it tends to scorch in the bread machine and should be baked in the oven. The figs should marinate in the rum at least 30 minutes or as long as overnight.

1lb LOAF	INGREDIENTS	1½lb LOAF
2 tbsp	rum	3 tbsp
⅓ cup	coarsely chopped figs	½ cup
1	egg	1 + 1 yolk
½ cup	milk	⅔ cup
1 tsp	vanilla extract	1½ tsp
1 tbsp	butter	1½ tbsp
2 tbsp	honey	3 tbsp
½ tsp	salt	¾ tsp
2 cups	bread flour	3 cups
1½ tsp	yeast	2¼ tsp

METHOD

Pour the rum over the chopped figs and set aside to marinate at least 30 minutes.

Put figs and remaining ingredients in bread pan in order suggested by your bread machine instructions. Set for dough. Press Start.

When dough is ready, punch it down on a lightly floured board. Let it rest a few minutes. Butter a 9½-inch loaf pan (pan can be smaller for the smaller recipe). Shape the dough into a loaf and put it in the pan, turning so all sides are buttered. Cover and let rise in a warm place for 1 hour.

When bread has risen, bake it in a preheated 350°F oven until the top is golden, about 30 to 45 minutes.

DATE WALNUT PASTRIES

This recipe makes yeast turnovers with a tangy date-walnut filling.

MAKES 10	INGREDIENTS	MAKES 15
	DOUGH	
²⁄₃ cup	milk	1 cup
¼ cup	brown sugar	6 tbsp
¼ cup	butter	6 tbsp
½ tsp	salt	¾ tsp
2 cups	bread flour	3 cups
1½ tsp	yeast	2¼ tsp
	FILLING	
2 tbsp	butter	3 tbsp
⅓ cup	all-purpose or bread flour	½ cup
2 tbsp	brown sugar	3 tbsp
½ tsp	cinnamon	¾ tsp
¼ cup	chopped walnuts	6 tbsp
⅓ cup	chopped dates	½ cup
	TOPPING	
2 tbsp	milk	3 tbsp
1 tbsp	sugar	1½ tbsp
¼ tsp	cinnamon	½ tsp

METHOD

Put dough ingredients in bread pan in order suggested by your bread machine instructions. Set for white bread, dough stage. Press Start.

While dough is rising, make filling. Melt butter in small skillet. Add flour, sugar, and cinnamon and stir until it forms a paste. Remove from heat and stir in walnuts and dates. Let cool.

Butter one or two baking sheets.

When dough is ready, remove from bread pan and punch down on floured surface. The dough will be soft and sticky. Roll into a thick log and cut into 10 pieces for the smaller recipe, 15 pieces for the larger recipe. Roll each piece into an oval ⅛ inch thick. Put some of the filling on half of each oval, fold the other half over and pinch each turnover closed. Place on the baking sheets. Lightly brush the top of each turnover with milk. Combine the cinnamon and sugar and sprinkle over the top of the pastries. Put in a warm place to rise for 1 hour.

Bake in a preheated 350°F oven until golden brown, for 20 to 25 minutes.

CALIFORNIA FRUIT BRAID

Filled with dates, figs, and dried apricots, this bread has a natural sweetness.
Twisted into a braid, it makes an impressive appearance at a brunch or luncheon.

1lb LOAF	INGREDIENTS	1½lb LOAF
⅓ cup	water	½ cup
⅓ cup	milk	½ cup
2 tbsp	butter	3 tbsp
2 tbsp	brown sugar	3 tbsp
½ tsp	ground nutmeg	¾ tsp
1 tsp	grated orange zest	1½ tsp
1 tsp	salt	1½ tsp
2 cups	bread flour	3 cups
1½ tsp	yeast	2¼ tsp
3 tbsp	chopped dried apricots	4½ tbsp
3 tbsp	chopped dates	4½ tbsp
3 tbsp	chopped figs	4½ tbsp

TOPPING

1 egg, beaten with a fork
1 tsp water
1–2 tbsp sugar

METHOD

Put all dough ingredients except fruits in bread pan in order suggested by your bread machine instructions. Set for dough. Press Start. After about 15 minutes or when the beeper signals time to add fruit, add apricots, dates and figs.

When dough is ready, punch it down on a lightly floured board. Let it rest a few minutes, then cut it into three equal pieces. Take each piece between your hands and roll it into a rope, about 15 inches long for the smaller loaf, 18 to 20 inches for the larger. Lay the three ropes on a nonstick or lightly buttered baking sheet.

Beginning at one end, pinch the ends together and braid the three ropes, then pinch the bottom ends together. Make a wash of the egg and water and brush it over the bread. Sprinkle lightly with sugar. Cover and let rise until bread has doubled in bulk, 45 to 60 minutes.

Place in a preheated 375°F oven and bake until the top is golden brown, about 30 to 45 minutes.

APPLE BRAID

This luscious coffee-time cake is pretty and smells like apple pie. It can be filled and braided, then left in the refrigerator overnight. In the morning, bring to room temperature, let rise and bake. My favorite apples for the filling are green Pippins or Granny Smiths, but other apples can be used.

1lb LOAF	INGREDIENTS	1½lb LOAF
½ cup	milk	⅔ cup
1	egg	2
3 tbsp	butter	4½ tbsp
¼ cup	sugar	6 tbsp
½ tsp	salt	¾ tsp
2 cups	bread flour	3 cups
2 tsp	yeast	1 tbsp
2 tbsp	confectioner's sugar	3 tbsp

	FILLING	
1½	apples	2
1 tsp	flour	1½ tsp
2 tbsp	sugar	3 tbsp
½ tsp	cinnamon	¾ tsp
½ tsp	vanilla extract	¾ tsp
½ tsp	lemon juice	¾ tsp
2 tbsp	raisins	3 tbsp

METHOD

Put all dough ingredients except confectioner's sugar in bread pan in order suggested by your bread machine instructions. Set for white bread, dough stage. Press Start.

While dough is rising, prepare the filling. Peel, core and chop the apples into ¼-inch dice. Toss with remaining ingredients.

When dough is ready, punch it down on a lightly floured board. Let it rest a few minutes. Butter a large baking sheet. Roll out the dough into a rectangle, ⅓ inch thick, and place on the baking sheet. With the dull side of a knife blade, mark – but do not cut – the rectangle into thirds. Spread the filling along the middle third.

Use the knife to cut the outer thirds diagonally into strips 1 inch wide. Bring up the two ends of the middle third just slightly to form an edge, then at either end, cross the two strips on either side over the middle. Working from one end of the braid to the other, cross alternating strips over the middle.

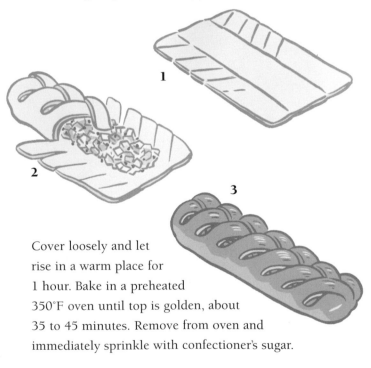

Cover loosely and let rise in a warm place for 1 hour. Bake in a preheated 350°F oven until top is golden, about 35 to 45 minutes. Remove from oven and immediately sprinkle with confectioner's sugar.

RAISED DOUGHNUTS

*Coated in sugar or drizzled with a sugar glaze, these doughnuts
are delicious.*

MAKES 8-10	INGREDIENTS	MAKES 12-15
½ cup	milk	⅞ cup
1	egg	1
2 tbsp	butter	3 tbsp
¼ cup	sugar	6 tbsp
½ tsp	salt	¾ tsp
2 cups	bread flour	3 cups
1½ tsp	yeast	2¼ tsp
	oil for frying	

CHOICE OF SUGAR COATINGS

confectioner's sugar
granulated cinnamon and sugar
sugar glaze (see below)

SUGAR GLAZE

¾ cup confectioner's sugar
½ tsp vanilla
1 tbsp warm milk

METHOD

Put all ingredients except oil and sugar coating in
bread pan in order suggested by your bread machine
instructions. Set for white bread, dough stage.
Press Start.

When dough is ready, punch down. Let it rest about
5 minutes. Then, on a lightly floured surface, roll dough
into a rectangle about ⅜ inch thick. Using a doughnut
cutter or a 3-inch cookie cutter, cut out doughnuts. If
you are not using a doughnut cutter, cut out a ½-inch
hole in the center. Knead scraps together and let rest 5
minutes. Reroll the dough and cut out more doughnuts.
Place the doughnuts on ungreased baking sheets. Cover
loosely and put them in a warm place to rise 45 minutes
to 1 hour, until doubled in bulk.

About 15 minutes before doughnuts finish rising, pour
oil at least 3 inches deep into a deep skillet, wok, or
saucepan. Heat oil to 365°F. Watch the oil temperature
carefully, as it can climb quickly. Slide two or three
doughnuts into the hot oil. Do not crowd them. Cook
until golden on the bottom, 1½ to 2½ minutes. Then
turn and cook the other side.

When doughnuts are golden, remove them from the oil,
letting them drain for a few moments over the oil. Then
put them on several layers of paper towels. Make sure
the oil temperature returns to 365°F before you add the
next batch of doughnuts.

Put confectioner's sugar or a mixture of cinnamon and
granulated sugar in a paper bag with two doughnuts.
Shake until they are coated. Remove and repeat until all
doughnuts are coated.

Alternatively, mix the ingredients for the sugar glaze
together and drizzle it over the tops of the doughnuts.

CALAS

Calas are rice fritters made with a yeast dough and fried like small doughnuts. The grains of cooked rice disappear into the delicious puffs of fried dough.

MAKES 30	INGREDIENTS	MAKES 45
2	eggs	3
2 tsp	vanilla	1 tbsp
6 tbsp	sugar	½ cup
½ tsp	salt	¼ tsp
½ tsp	nutmeg	¼ tsp
½ tsp	grated lemon peel	¼ tsp
2 cups	cooked, cooled rice	3 cups
2 cups	bread flour	3 cups
1 tsp	yeast	1½ tsp
	oil for frying	
	confectioner's sugar	

METHOD

Put all ingredients except oil and confectioner's sugar in bread pan in order suggested by your bread machine instructions. Set for white bread, dough stage. Press Start.

When dough is ready, punch down. Let it rest about 5 minutes. Then cut off walnut-sized pieces and place them on a greased baking sheet. (Lightly flour your hands, if necessary, to work with the sticky batter.) Cover loosely and put them in a warm place to rise for 1 hour.

Pour oil at least 3 inches deep into a deep skillet, wok, or saucepan. Heat oil to 365°F. Watch the oil temperature carefully, as it can climb quickly. Slide a few rice balls into the hot oil. Do not crowd them. They will bob back up to the surface. Cook until golden on the bottom, about 2 minutes. Then turn and cook another 2 minutes on the other side.

When fritters are golden, remove them from the oil, letting them drain for a few moments over the oil. Then put them on several layers of paper towels. Sprinkle them with confectioner's sugar. Calas should be served warm. You may put the cooked calas in a warm oven while others are cooking. Make sure the oil temperature returns to 365°F before you add the next batch of calas.

LEMON POPPYSEED BRAID

*Slightly sweet, flavored with lemon, and full of poppy seeds, this braided
bread makes an impressive appearance at brunch or tea.*

1 lb LOAF	INGREDIENTS	1½ lb LOAF
1	egg	1 egg + 1 yolk
½ cup	lemon yogurt	¾ cup
3 tbsp	butter	4½ tbsp
3 tbsp	sugar	4½ tbsp
3 tbsp	poppy seeds	4½ tbsp
2 tsp	grated lemon peel	1 tbsp
1 tsp	salt	1½ tsp
2 cups	bread flour	3 cups
1½ tsp	yeast	2¼ tsp

GLAZE

1 egg white beaten with 2 tsp water

METHOD

Put all dough ingredients in bread machine pan. Set for
white or sweet bread, dough stage. Press Start.

When dough is ready, remove from pan and punch
down. Cut into three equal pieces. Let it rest 5 minutes.
Butter a baking sheet. Roll each piece of dough into a
rope, about 14 inches for smaller loaf, 18 to 20 inches
for larger loaf. Braid three ropes together and tuck ends
under. Cover dough and put in a warm place to rise
until doubled, 45 minutes to 1 hour.

Brush dough with egg-water wash. Bake bread in a
preheated 350°F oven until golden, 25 to 30 minutes.

BANANA DATE MONKEY BREAD

This is a very sweet pull-apart bread, loved by children, and delicious for breakfast.

1lb LOAF	INGREDIENTS	1½lb LOAF
½ cup	plain yogurt	¾ cup
⅓ cup	mashed banana	½ cup
¼ cup	chopped dates	6 tbsp
1 tbsp	water	1½ tbsp
2 tbsp	butter	3 tbsp
2 tbsp	honey	3 tbsp
½ tsp	salt	¾ tsp
½ tsp	ground nutmeg	¾ tsp
2 cups	bread flour	3 cups
1½ tsp	yeast	2¼ tsp

DIPPING

1lb LOAF	INGREDIENTS	1½lb LOAF
2 tbsp	rum (see below)	3 tbsp
3 tbsp	melted butter	4½ tbsp
½ cup	sugar	¾ cup
½ cup	brown sugar	¾ cup
½ tsp	cinnamon	¾ tsp
½ tsp	ground nutmeg	¾ tsp

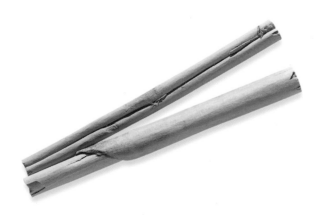

TIP

You may substitute rum flavoring, vanilla extract or orange juice for the rum.

METHOD

Put dough ingredients in bread pan in order suggested by your bread machine instructions. Set for white bread, dough stage. Press Start.

Lightly butter a baking dish. A 10-inch Bundt pan or tube pan works well for both sizes, or use a round casserole dish. Stir the rum or other flavoring into the melted butter. In another bowl, mix the sugars, cinnamon and nutmeg, then put about half the sugar mixture in a separate bowl.

When dough is ready, punch down. Roll dough into a thick log and cut into 24 pieces for the smaller loaf, 30 to 36 pieces for the larger loaf. Roll each piece into a ball; it does not need to be perfectly round. Dip each ball in butter-rum mix, then in sugar mix. As the butter drips into the sugar mix, it will become difficult to work with, so add a little sugar mix from the reserve bowl. Layer the sugared balls into the baking pan so they are close but not touching; they need room to rise. With each succeeding layer, place balls so they overlap empty spaces below. When the dough is layered, pour any remaining butter-rum mix and sugar over the loaf.

Cover the baking pan loosely and put it in a warm place to rise until doubled in volume, about 45 minutes. Or at this point you can put the assembled loaf in the refrigerator, where it will rise very slowly. The next morning, or when you are ready to bake, let loaf return to room temperature and finish rising.

Bake in a preheated 350°F oven until bread is lightly browned and a skewer inserted in the bread comes out clean, 25 to 40 minutes. Invert bread on to a serving plate, being very careful of any hot syrup that has collected in the bottom of the pan. Let cool just long enough that the sugar syrup is not burning hot, and serve.

ORANGE MONKEY BREAD

This sweet pull-apart bread is a favorite breakfast treat. Small balls of sweet, orange-flavored dough are dipped in a melted butter seasoned with orange liqueur, dipped in cinnamon and sugar, and layered in a baking pan. The bread is wonderful when warm, but still tastes good at room temperature. Time the making of the bread so it comes out of the oven 10 to 15 minutes before meal time.

1 lb LOAF	INGREDIENTS	1½ lb LOAF
⅔ cup	milk	1 cup
2 tbsp	butter	3 tbsp
2 tbsp	sugar	3 tbsp
½ tsp	salt	¾ tsp
2 tsp	grated orange peel	1 tbsp
2 cups	bread flour	3 cups
1½ tsp	yeast	2¼ tsp
3 tbsp	melted butter	4½ tbsp
2 tbsp	orange liqueur or orange juice	3 tbsp
1 cup	sugar	1½ cups
1 tsp	cinnamon	1½ tsp

METHOD

Put first seven ingredients in bread pan in order suggested by your bread machine instructions. Set for white or sweet bread, dough stage. Press Start.

Lightly butter baking dish. A few minutes before dough is ready, melt butter. Stir in orange juice or orange liqueur. In a separate bowl, mix the cinnamon and sugar. Put about half of the cinnamon and sugar in another bowl. Each time you dip a buttery ball into the sugar, it will drip a little of the butter into the sugar, and the sugar will become hard to work with. Then replenish it with some of the reserved cinnamon and sugar.

Remove the dough from the bread machine and punch down. Roll dough into a thick log and cut it into 20 to 24 pieces for the small loaf, 30 to 36 pieces for the large loaf. Roll pieces of dough into balls (they do not need to be perfectly round). Dip each ball in butter-orange mixture, then in cinnamon-sugar and layer in baking pan. Note: the pieces in the first layer should be close but not touching to give them room to rise. On each succeeding layer, place balls so they overlap empty spaces on the layer beneath. You can put the assembled bread in the refrigerator the night before, and it will rise a little overnight. Let the dough return to room temperature and finish rising, then bake. Monkey bread is traditionally baked in a tube pan, 10 inches across for the larger loaf, a 7- or 8-inch pan for the smaller loaf. However, it looks impressive and tastes just as good when baked in round casserole dishes, about 1 inch smaller in diameter than the tube pans.

Drizzle any remaining butter and cinnamon-sugar over the dough in the pan. Cover it loosely, and put it in a warm place to rise. When bread has doubled in volume, about 30 to 40 minutes, put it in preheated 350°F oven. Bake until bread is lightly browned and a skewer inserted in the bread comes out clean, about 25 to 30 minutes. Invert bread on serving plate, being very careful of the hot syrup that has collected at the bottom of the pan. (Drain off excess syrup first, if desired, or let the syrup run onto the plate.) Remove baking pan, let it cool a little, and serve.

GRANDMA'S CINNAMON RAISIN ROLLS

My grandmother, Letty Belden, has made these delicious rolls by hand in huge batches for years. She gladly shared her recipe, which I have cut down in size and converted for use in a bread machine.

MAKES 12	INGREDIENTS	MAKES 18
1	egg	1 + 1 yolk
⅓ cup	mashed potatoes	½ cup
3 tbsp	milk	4½ tbsp
3 tbsp	butter	4½ tbsp
3 tbsp	sugar	4½ tbsp
½ tsp	salt	¾ tsp
½ tsp	baking powder	¾ tsp
¼ tsp	baking soda	½ tsp
2 cups	bread flour	3 cups
1½ tsp	yeast	2¼ tsp
2 tbsp	very soft butter	3 tbsp
3 tbsp	brown sugar	4½ tbsp
1 tsp	cinnamon	1½ tsp
⅓ cup	raisins	½ cup

ICING

1 cup	confectioner's sugar	1½ cups
1 tbsp	milk	1½ tbsp
¼ tsp	vanilla extract	½ tsp

METHOD

Put all but last four dough ingredients in bread pan in order suggested by your bread machine instructions. Set for white bread, dough stage. Press Start.

When dough is ready, punch it down on a lightly floured board. Let it rest a few minutes, then roll it out into a rectangle about 10 x 15 inches for the smaller recipe, about 15 x 15 inches for the larger one. Spread the soft butter over the dough. Mix the brown sugar and cinnamon and sprinkle over the dough. Sprinkle the raisins over the sugar.

Starting at a long end, roll the dough into a tight cylinder. Trim the uneven ends. Cut into ¾-inch slices. Place slightly apart on one or two buttered baking sheets. Cover, put in a warm place and let rise until doubled in bulk, about 1 hour.

With your fingertip, gently press any exposed raisins back into folds of dough. Bake rolls in a preheated 350°F oven until golden brown, 20 to 25 minutes. While rolls are still warm, make icing by mixing confectioner's sugar, milk and vanilla. Spread icing over the tops of rolls and allow some to drip down sides.

NOTE

This recipe is based on pure mashed potatoes with no additions. If milk or other liquids have been added to the potatoes, check during kneading and add a little flour if dough is too wet.

TUSCAN SWEET BREAD

This crusty oven-baked bread brings together a delicious mélange of orange, rum, and fennel. It is good for breakfast or tea. Baked in a ring and decoratively slashed, it makes a pretty centerpiece.

1lb LOAF	INGREDIENTS	1½lb LOAF
1	egg	1 + 1 yolk
3 tbsp	milk	4½ tbsp
¼ cup	water	6 tbsp
1 tsp	rum	1½ tsp
2 tbsp	butter	3 tbsp
3 tbsp	sugar	4½ tbsp
1 tsp	grated orange zest	1½ tsp
1 tsp	fennel seeds	1½ tsp
1 tsp	salt	1½ tsp
1⅓ cups	bread flour	2 cups
⅔ cup	semolina flour	1 cup
1½ tsp	yeast	2¼ tsp
3 tbsp	golden raisins	4½ tbsp

TOPPING

1 egg yolk

1 tsp rum

1½–2 tsp sugar

METHOD

Put all dough ingredients except raisins in bread pan in order suggested by your bread machine instructions. Set for dough. Press Start. After about 15 minutes or when the beeper signals time to add fruit, add raisins.

When dough is ready, punch it down on a lightly floured board. Let it rest a few minutes. Then take it between your hands and roll it into a rope, about 15 inches long for the smaller loaf, 18 to 20 inches for the larger. Put it on a lightly buttered baking sheet. Bring the ends together to form a circle. Cover and let rise 45 to 60 minutes.

Lightly beat the egg yolk and rum. Paint onto the top of the bread and sprinkle with sugar. Cut diagonal slashes about 2 inches apart in the top. Bake in a preheated 350°F oven until golden brown, 35 to 55 minutes.

CINNAMON RAISIN SWIRL BREAD

This is an easy breakfast bread that tastes like cinnamon rolls, although it is not as gooey. It is delicious warm and doesn't need butter. The bread can be assembled the night before, then left to rise in the refrigerator overnight.

1 lb LOAF	INGREDIENTS	1½ lb LOAF
¾ cup	milk	1¼ cups
1 tbsp	butter	1½ tbsp
3 tbsp	sugar	4½ tbsp
1 tsp	salt	1½ tsp
2 cups	bread flour	3 cups
2 tsp	yeast	1 tbsp
¼ cup	raisins	6 tbsp
1½ tbsp	very soft butter	2 tbsp
¼ cup	brown sugar	6 tbsp
1 tsp	cinnamon	1½ tsp

METHOD

Put first six ingredients in bread pan in order suggested by your bread machine instructions. Set for white or sweet bread, dough stage. Press Start. Add the raisins after the first kneading or when the beep sounds to add fruit.

Remove butter from refrigerator to soften it. Mix brown sugar and cinnamon. Butter a 9½-inch loaf pan (large enough for either recipe).

Remove dough from bread machine and punch down. Let it rest 5 minutes. Roll it out on a lightly floured surface to form a rectangle about 8 inches wide and about 16 inches long. Spread the butter, then sprinkle the brown sugar mixture over the surface of the dough. Roll it into a fat 8-inch-long cylinder. Tucking the edge under, put it in the loaf pan. Loosely cover and put in a warm place to rise for 1 hour.

Bake the loaf in a preheated 350°F oven until top is golden and a skewer inserted in the bread comes out clean, 25 to 30 minutes. Remove the bread from the pan and put it on a wire rack. Let it cool at least 30 minutes so the hot sugar does not burn you.

PRUNE YOGURT BREAKFAST CRESCENTS

Prunes give the dough of these breakfast treats sweetness and moisture. The chopped prunes are added at the beginning so that they are puréed during the kneading and are well incorporated into the dough.

MAKES 16	INGREDIENTS	MAKES 24
⅔ cup	plain yogurt	1 cup
1	egg	1 + 1 yolk
⅓ cup	chopped dried prunes	½ cup
2 tbsp	butter	3 tbsp
2 tbsp	sugar	3 tbsp
1 tsp	salt	1½ tsp
2 cups	bread flour	3 cups
1½ tsp	yeast	2¼ tsp

	FILLING	
2 tbsp	very soft butter	3 tbsp
⅓ cup	brown sugar	½ cup
1 tsp	cinnamon	1½ tsp
½ cup	finely chopped pecans	¾ cup

METHOD

Put dough ingredients in bread pan in order suggested by your bread machine instructions. Set for white bread, dough stage. Press Start.

When dough is ready, punch it down on a lightly floured board. Cut the smaller recipe into two equal pieces, the larger recipe into three. Let it rest a few minutes. Butter two baking sheets, then roll each piece into a circle about 8 inches in diameter. Spread the soft butter over the dough. Mix the brown sugar and cinnamon and sprinkle over the butter. Sprinkle the pecans over the sugar.

Cut each circle into 8 wedges. Starting from the outside of the circle, loosely roll up each wedge, working toward the point. Stretch slightly and pull into a curve. Set each crescent on baking sheet, with the point underneath.

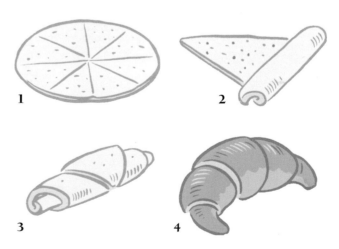

1 2

3 4

Cover, put in a warm place and let rise until doubled in size, about 1 hour. Bake in a preheated 375°F oven for 12 to 15 minutes.

9

Breads from around the World

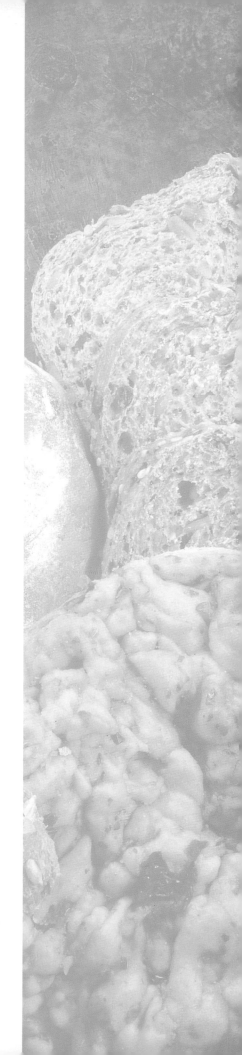

BOLILLOS

These Mexican rolls are large and crusty, excellent with dinner.

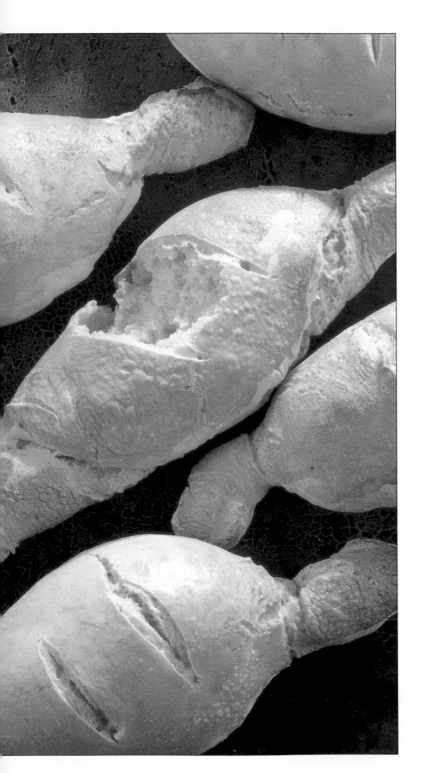

MAKES 6	INGREDIENTS	MAKES 9
⅔ cup	water	1 cup
1 tsp	sugar	1½ tsp
1 tsp	salt	1½ tsp
2 cups	bread flour	3 cups
1½ tsp	yeast	2¼ tsp

GLAZE

1 egg

1 tbsp water

METHOD

Put all ingredients except glaze in bread pan in order suggested by your bread machine instructions. Set for white bread, dough stage. Press Start.

Lightly oil a baking sheet.

When dough is ready, remove from bread machine and punch down. Cut smaller recipe into 6 equal pièces, the larger recipe into 9 pieces. Roll each piece into a ball. Flatten ball, then gently stretch and elongate to form an oval. Now, working on the long sides of the oval, fold those sides in toward the middle. Roll and stretch so the center is thick and the ends are tapered like a spindle. Place the rolls, seam side down, on the baking sheet. Cover loosely and set in a warm place to rise until doubled, about 1 hour.

Preheat oven to 400°F. Lightly brush rolls with egg glaze. With a sharp knife or razor blade, make two diagonal slashes in the top of each roll. Bake 15 to 20 minutes, until rolls are golden and crusty.

PITA BREAD

These rounds of dough puff up when they are baked at high temperature. Cut open an edge to create pockets that can be stuffed with all kinds of fillings.

MAKES 6	INGREDIENTS	MAKES 9
¾ cup	water	1¼ cups
1 tbsp	olive oil	1½ tbsp
1 tsp	sugar	1½ tsp
1 tsp	salt	1½ tsp
1⅓ cups	bread flour	2 cups
⅔ cup	whole-wheat flour	1 cup
1½ tsp	yeast	2¼ tsp

METHOD

Put ingredients in bread pan in order suggested by your bread machine instructions and set for whole-wheat, dough stage.

Punch down dough and cut into 6 equal pieces for smaller recipe, 9 pieces for the larger one. Roll each piece between your hands to form a ball. Flatten slightly and let dough rest about 10 minutes. This will let the dough relax so it will stretch more readily when you roll it out, rather than bouncing back. On a lightly floured surface, roll out each circle of dough to a diameter of about 6 inches. Use flour sparingly, as too much flour will interfere with the moisture that creates steam and causes the dough to puff up. Cover the dough with plastic wrap or a barely damp towel, and let the dough rise about 30 minutes, until it is puffy.

Preheat oven to 475°F. Lightly sprinkle cornmeal on a baking sheet. When dough is ready, carefully transfer rounds to the baking sheet. Bake until dough puffs up and is lightly browned, 5 to 6 minutes, then turn and bake until other side is lightly browned, about 2 minutes.

BRIOCHE

This buttery bread is not quite the same as the classic French brioche baked in a fluted pan, but is a deliciously close cousin. Although it makes good sandwiches, it is best served simply, toasted or untoasted, with butter.

1 lb LOAF	INGREDIENTS	1½ lb LOAF
¼ cup	water	6 tbsp
2	eggs	3
⅓ cup	butter	½ cup
1 tbsp	sugar	1½ tbsp
½ tsp	salt	¾ tsp
2 cups	bread flour	3 cups
1½ tsp	yeast	2¼ tsp

METHOD

Put ingredients in bread pan in order suggested by your bread machine instructions. It is crucial that the butter is softened to room temperature – not melted – when it is added to the other ingredients. Set for white bread, medium crust. Press Start.

PISTOLET

Pistolets are split rolls made in France and Belgium. Traditionally the dough is allowed to rise for several hours on the first rising to develop the flavor, then rise twice more. The dough is shaped into a plum-sized ball, then nearly split with the handle of a wooden spoon.

MAKES 15	INGREDIENTS	MAKES 22
¾ cup	water	1¼ cups
3 tbsp	powdered milk	4½ tbsp
2 tbsp	butter	3 tbsp
1 tbsp	sugar	1½ tbsp
1 tsp	salt	1½ tsp
2 cups	bread flour	3 cups
1½ tsp	yeast	2¼ tsp
¼ cup	rye flour	⅓ cup

METHOD

Put all ingredients except rye flour in bread pan in order suggested by your bread machine instructions. Set for white bread, dough stage. Press Start.

If your machine does not punch down the dough for you at this point, or if you can stop the machine, remove the pan. Cover it loosely, put it in a warm place and let dough continue rising for another two hours. It will have tripled in volume, and yeast flavors will have developed.

Punch the dough down and let it rise again for 45 minutes. Butter a baking sheet.

When dough is ready, punch it down. Cut smaller recipe into about 15 equal pieces, the larger recipe into about 22 pieces. Roll each piece into a ball. Dust the top with rye flour. Oil the dowel-like wooden handle of a large spoon. Use the handle to split each ball almost in half. The two sides of the ball should still be connected by a narrow strip of dough. Hold each pistolet at each end of the split with your thumbs in the trough. Pull gently to elongate the roll, and the sides will almost come together.

Traditionally, the roll is placed top (seam-side) down on the baking sheet. After it has risen, it is turned upright and baked. However, if you are all thumbs and tend to deflate the dough when you handle it, just leave it upright and let it rise with the seam side up. Cover them up loosely, put in a warm place, and let them rise for 30 minutes.

Preheat oven to 425°F. Pour boiling water into a shallow baking pan and place it on the bottom shelf of the oven. The steam will give the pistolets a crusty finish. Bake pistolets until they are golden brown and crusty, 15 to 20 minutes.

PORTUGUESE SWEET BREAD

This is an eggy, light-textured sweet bread, flavored with vanilla, lemon, and nutmeg. It used to be eaten as an Easter bread in Portugal, but now is eaten as a breakfast bread year-round.

1 lb LOAF	INGREDIENTS	1½ lb LOAF
2	eggs	3
⅓ cup	milk	½ cup
2 tbsp	butter	3 tbsp
3 tbsp	sugar	4½ tbsp
½ tsp	salt	¾ tsp
1 tsp	vanilla	1½ tsp
2 tsp	grated lemon peel	1 tbsp
½ tsp	nutmeg	¾ tsp
2 cups	bread flour	3 cups
1½ tsp	yeast	2¼ tsp

METHOD

Put ingredients in bread pan in order suggested by your bread machine instructions. Set for white or sweet bread, light crust. Press Start.

FOCCACIO

Serve wedges of this hearty bread as an hors d'oeuvre or with a meal instead of garlic bread. Instead of butter, dip pieces in high-quality olive oil. This bread is best served warm.

1 lb LOAF	INGREDIENTS	1½ lb LOAF
⅔ cup	water	1 cup
2 tbsp	olive oil	3 tbsp
1 tsp	salt	1½ tsp
2 cups	bread flour	3 cups
1¼ tsp	yeast	2 tsp
1 or 2	minced garlic cloves	2 or 3
1 tsp	dried rosemary	1½ tsp
1 tsp	coarse salt	1½ tsp
2 tbsp	olive oil	3 tbsp
2 tsp	grated Parmesan	1 tbsp

METHOD

Put first five ingredients in bread pan in order suggested by your bread machine instructions. Set for white bread, dough stage. Press Start.

Preheat oven to 400°F. Lightly sprinkle cornmeal on a baking sheet.

Remove dough and punch down. Let dough rest about 5 minutes. On a lightly floured surface, roll dough into a round, about ½ inch thick. Place dough on baking sheet. Sprinkle the garlic, rosemary, and coarse salt over the top, then lightly press it into the dough. With your fingertips, poke shallow indentations all over the top of the round. Pour the remaining olive oil over the top, letting it pool in the indentations. Sprinkle Parmesan over the top.

Bake bread until lightly browned, about 20 minutes.

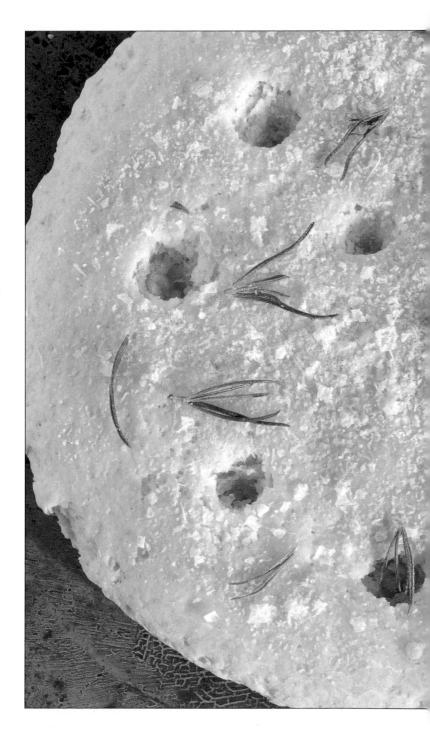

PULLA

Pulla is a Finnish sweet bread seasoned with cardamom, a spice widely used in Scandinavian cooking. It is an everyday bread in Finland, often dressed up with raisins and candied orange peel for holiday celebrations.

1 lb LOAF	INGREDIENTS	1½ lb LOAF
1	egg	1 + 1 yolk
½ cup	milk	¾ cup
2 tbsp	butter	3 tbsp
3 tbsp	sugar	4½ tbsp
½ tsp	salt	¾ tsp
1 tsp	ground cardamom	1½ tsp
2 cups	bread flour	3 cups
2 tsp	yeast	1 tbsp

GLAZE

1 egg white beaten with 2 tsp water
2 tbsp sliced or slivered almonds
1–2 tbsp sugar

METHOD

Put all dough ingredients in bread machine pan. Set for white or sweet bread, dough stage. Press Start.

When dough is ready, take out and punch down. Cut into three equal pieces. Let it rest 5 minutes. Butter a baking sheet. Roll each piece into a rope, about 16 inches for smaller loaf, 20 inches for larger loaf. Braid the ropes, tucking ends under. Cover dough and put in a warm place to rise until doubled.

Brush dough with egg-water wash. Sprinkle with almonds and then with sugar. Bake bread in preheated 375°F oven until golden, about 35 minutes.

VERTERKAKE

This dense, sweet Norwegian bread takes its name from verterol, one of the ingredients in a Norwegian non-alcoholic beer. You can use alcoholic or non-alcoholic beer. This bread, adapted from a James Beard recipe, produces a soft dough that does not cook evenly in the bread machine, so it is baked in a conventional oven.

1 lb LOAF	INGREDIENTS	1½ lb LOAF
½ cup	flat dark beer	¾ cup
⅓ cup	milk	½ cup
2 tbsp	corn syrup	3 tbsp
2 tbsp	sugar	3 tbsp
¼ tsp	ground cloves	½ tsp
¼ tsp	black pepper	½ tsp
½ tsp	salt	¾ tsp
1¼ cups	bread flour	1¾ cups
1 cup	rye flour	1½ cups
1½ tsp	yeast	2¼ tsp
2 tbsp	raisins	3 tbsp

METHOD

Put all ingredients except raisins in bread pan in order suggested by your bread machine instructions. Set for whole-wheat bread, dough stage. Press Start. Add raisins after first kneading or when the machine beeps that it is time to add fruit.

Oil an 8½- to 9½-inch bread pan for the smaller loaf, a 9½- to 10½-inch pan for the larger loaf.

When dough is ready, remove it from the bread machine and punch down. Shape it into a loaf. Place it in the bread pan, then turn so all sides of the dough are oiled. Cover loosely, set it in a warm place, and let it rise until doubled in bulk, 45 minutes to 1 hour.

Brush loaf with hot water and lightly prick the surface with a toothpick. Bake bread in a preheated 375°F oven until loaf browns and sounds hollow when thumped, 35 to 45 minutes.

ITALIAN SAUSAGE BREAD

This bread is wrapped around a substantial filling of sausage, cheese, pine nuts and onion. It makes a great snack for watching football – or serve it with a vegetable soup or minestrone.

450 g (1 lb) LOAF	INGREDIENTS	675 g (1½ lb) LOAF
120 ml (4 fl oz)	milk	175 ml (6 fl oz)
4 tbsp	water	6 tbsp
1 tbsp	butter	1½ tbsp
1 tbsp	sugar	1½ tbsp
1 tsp	dried basil	1½ tsp
½ tsp	dried oregano	¾ tsp
1 tsp	salt	1½ tsp
270 g (10 oz)	bread flour	425 g (15 oz)
1½ tsp	yeast	2¼ tsp

	FILLING	
225 g (8 oz)	Italian sausage	350 g (12 oz)
25 g (1 oz)	finely chopped onion	40 g (1½ oz)
1	clove garlic, chopped	1 or 2
2 tbsp	pine kernels	3 tbsp
1	egg, lightly beaten	1
175 g (6 oz)	grated mozzarella	275 g (9 oz)

METHOD

Put dough ingredients in bread tin in order suggested by your bread machine instructions. Set for white bread, dough stage. Press Start.

While the dough is working, make the filling. Crumble the sausage into a hot frying pan and cook, stirring often, until sausage is browned. Drain and remove sausage. Chop the sausage into small bits. Discard all but 1 tablespoon of fat.

Reheat the fat and sauté onion, garlic and pine nuts for 5 minutes. Combine the onion mixture with the cooked sausage. When mixture has cooled slightly, add the egg and mix well.

When dough is ready, punch it down on a lightly floured board. Let it rest a few minutes. Butter a 25-cm (9½-inch) loaf tin. Roll the dough out into a rectangle no wider than the length of the bread tin. Gently spread the sausage filling over the surface of the bread, taking care not to tear the dough. Sprinkle the mozzarella over the filling. Starting at the short end, roll dough into a cylinder. If necessary, turn ends under. Put the dough into the bread tin, seam side down. Cover and let rise in a warm place for 1 hour.

Bake in a preheated 180°C/350°F/Gas 4 oven until golden, about 35 to 40 minutes. Let cool slightly, then slice and serve while warm.

TIP

If you use freshly grated cheese, pack it tightly or much of the measurement will be air.

SWEDISH LIMPA BREAD

This is a a slightly sweet rye bread, flavored with a delicious combination of orange peel, anise seed, and caraway seed. It can be used for sandwiches or canapés, but I like it best with only sweet butter.

1 lb LOAF	INGREDIENTS	1½ lb LOAF
¾ cup	water	1¼ cups
1 tbsp	vegetable oil	1½ tbsp
2 tbsp	honey	3 tbsp
1 tsp	salt	1½ tsp
½ tsp	anise seed	¾ tsp
½ tsp	caraway seeds	¾ tsp
1 tbsp	grated orange peel	1½ tbsp
1½ cups	bread flour	2¼ cups
¾ cup	rye flour	1¼ cups
1½ tsp	yeast	2¼ tsp

METHOD

Put ingredients in bread pan in order suggested by your bread machine instructions. Set for whole-wheat bread, medium crust. Press Start.

SAVORY KUGELHOPF

The kugelhopf is a rich Austrian bread for special occasions. Traditionally it is a sweet bread loaded with fruit, but this version is a savory bread, made with bacon, cheese, and onions. Eat it as an accompaniment to soup and salad. Made with extra egg and butter, it cannot be baked in the bread machine. The kugelhopf has its own special pan, but can be baked in a Bundt pan or tube pan.

1lb LOAF	INGREDIENTS	1½lb LOAF
2 + 1 yolk	eggs	4
¼ cup	milk	⅓ cup
¼ cup	butter	6 tbsp
1 tbsp	sugar	1½ tbsp
½ tsp	dried thyme	¾ tsp
¼ tsp	fresh-ground black pepper	½ tsp
1 tsp	salt	1½ tsp
2 cups	bread flour	3 cups
2 tsp	yeast	1 tbsp
4 slices	bacon	6 slices
⅓ cup	chopped onion	½ cup
⅓ cup	shredded Swiss cheese, packed	½ cup

METHOD

Put all but last three ingredients in bread pan in order suggested by your bread machine instructions. Set wheat dough. Press Start.

Meanwhile, dice the bacon and cook until crisp. Remove bacon, drain on paper towels, and let cool. Pour off all but a few teaspoons of bacon grease. Reheat the grease and add the onion. Sauté for 10 minutes. Remove from heat, drain, and let cool.

Butter a 9-cup tube pan for either size loaf, or a 6-cup pan can be used for the smaller loaf.

When dough is ready, remove from bread machine, punch down on a lightly floured surface, then let rest a few minutes. Gradually knead in the bacon, onions, and cheese. Roll dough between your hands to make a thick log and put it in the pan, stretching or shaping as needed. Cover and put in a warm place to rise for 45 minutes.

Bake Kugelhopf in a preheated 350°F oven until golden brown, about 35 to 45 minutes.

KUGELHOPF

This is an Austrian bread reputedly brought to France by Marie Antoinette. It is a sweet, fruit-studded batter bread and will not cook evenly in the bread machine, so must be baked in the oven. It is considered so special a bread that a fluted tube pan was created for it, but a bundt pan or angel-food cake pan will do nicely.

1 lb LOAF	INGREDIENTS	1½ lb LOAF
2 + 1 yolk	eggs	4 eggs
3 tbsp	milk	⅓ cup
⅓ cup	butter	½ cup
3½ tbsp	sugar	⅓ cup
½ tsp	vanilla	1 tsp
2 tsp	grated lemon peel	1 tbsp
½ tsp	salt	1 tsp
2 cups	bread flour	3 cups
2 tsp	yeast	1 tbsp
¼ cup	raisins	¾ cup
⅓ cup	slivered almonds	½ cup

confectioner's sugar

METHOD

Put all ingredients except raisins, almonds, and confectioner's sugar in bread pan in order suggested by your bread machine instructions. Set for white or sweet bread, dough stage. Press Start. Add raisins and almonds at the beeper or after the first kneading.

Remove the dough from the bread machine and punch down. Let it rest for 5 minutes. Butter a 6-cup tube pan for the smaller loaf, a 9-cup tube pan for the larger loaf. Put the dough in the pan and spread it around evenly. Cover loosely and put in a warm place to rise 45 minutes to 1 hour.

Bake kugelhopf in a preheated 350°F oven until a skewer inserted in bread comes out clean, 35 to 40 minutes. Let cool 10 minutes, then invert on cooling rack. Dust with confectioner's sugar while kugelhopf is still warm.

SCANDINAVIAN TEA RING
WITH APRICOT CHEESE FILLING

This pretty cake uses a sweet egg dough flavored with cardamom, preferably freshly ground. It is filled with a mixture of dried apricots and cream cheese.

1lb LOAF	INGREDIENTS	1½lb LOAF
1	egg	2
½ cup	milk	⅔ cup
3 tbsp	butter	4½ tbsp
2 tbsp	sugar	3 tbsp
1 tsp	ground cardamom	1½ tsp
1 tsp	salt	1½ tsp
2 cups	bread flour	3 cups
1½ tsp	yeast	2¼ tsp

	FILLING	
8 oz	cream cheese, at room temperature	12 oz
1	egg yolk	1
2 tbsp	sugar	3 tbsp
1 tsp	vanilla extract	1½ tsp
½ tsp	grated lemon zest	¾ tsp
½ tsp	ground cardamom	¾ tsp
⅓ cup	chopped dried apricots	½ cup

METHOD

Put dough ingredients in bread pan in order suggested by your bread machine instructions. Set for white bread, dough stage. Press Start.

While dough is rising, make the filling. Beat together the cream cheese and egg. Add sugar, vanilla, lemon, and cardamom and mix well. Add apricots. Do not refrigerate – the filling needs to be soft.

When dough is ready, punch it down on a lightly floured board. Let it rest a few minutes. Then roll it out into a rectangle about 10 x 15 inches for the smaller recipe, about 15 x 15 inches for the larger one. Spread the filling over the dough. Starting at a long end, roll the dough into a tight cylinder. Place the cylinder on a buttered baking sheet. Pull the ends together to form a circle. With a sharp knife, make cuts in the outside of the ring every ¾ inch, cutting about halfway through the dough. Do not slice all the way through. Cover, put in a warm place and let rise until doubled in bulk, about 1 hour.

1

2

3

Bake tea ring in a preheated 350°F oven until golden brown, 25 to 35 minutes.

4

NORWEGIAN CARDAMOM BREAD

*Fresh cardamom seeds are a delicious addition to a sweet bread and are
particularly popular in Scandinavian countries. Whole seedpods can sometimes be
found in the spice racks of well-stocked grocery stores. Break open the pods,
remove the tiny black seeds and grind them in a grinder or mortar and pestle.
Fresh cardamom is hard to find, and we usually must be satisfied with the milder
flavor of dried, ground cardamom. Here, we use it in a braided whole-wheat bread
that is full of golden raisins, dried apricots and almonds.*

1lb LOAF	INGREDIENTS	1½lb LOAF
1	egg	2
6 tbsp	milk	7 tbsp
2 tbsp	vegetable oil	3 tbsp
2 tbsp	honey	3 tbsp
1 tsp	salt	1½ tsp
1 tsp	ground cardamom	1½ tsp
⅔ cup	whole-wheat flour	1 cup
1⅓ cups	bread flour	2 cups
2 tsp	yeast	1 tbsp
¼ cup	chopped dried apricots	6 tbsp
¼ cup	golden raisins	6 tbsp
¼ cup	slivered almonds	6 tbsp

EGG WASH

1 egg, beaten with a fork
2 tsp water

METHOD

Put all dough ingredients except apricots, raisins, and
almonds in bread pan in order suggested by your bread
machine instructions. Set for whole-wheat dough. Press
Start. After about 15 minutes or when the beeper signals
time to add fruit, add raisins, apricots and nuts.

When dough is ready, punch it down on a lightly
floured board. Let it rest a few minutes, then cut it into
three equal pieces. Take each piece between your hands
and roll it into a rope, about 15 inches long for the
smaller loaf, 18 to 20 inches for the larger. Lay the three
ropes on a nonstick or lightly buttered baking sheet.
Beginning at one end, pinch the ends together and braid
the three ropes, then pinch the bottom ends together.
Make a wash of the egg and water and brush it over the
bread. Cover and let rise until bread has doubled in
bulk, 45 to 60 minutes.

Place in a preheated 375°F oven and bake until the top
is golden brown, 25 to 40 minutes.

ZEPPOLES

Zeppoles, also called zappla, are Italian doughnuts: small circles of fried dough.
For variety, add a pinch of grated lemon zest or a dash or nutmeg – or both.

MAKES 16	INGREDIENTS	MAKES 24
1	egg	2
¼ cup	water	¼ cup
⅓ cup	milk	½ cup
1 tsp	vanilla extract	1½ tsp
1 tbsp	butter	1½ tbsp
1 tbsp	sugar	1½ tbsp
½ tsp	salt	¾ tsp
2 cups	bread flour	3 cups
1½ tsp	yeast	2¼ tsp

vegetable oil for frying
confectioner's sugar

METHOD

Put all ingredients except oil and confectioner's sugar in bread pan in order suggested by your bread machine instructions. Set for dough. Press Start.

Lightly butter one or two baking sheets. When dough is ready, remove from bread pan, punch down on lightly floured surface and let rest a few minutes. Roll the dough into a fat log. Cut into 16 pieces for the smaller recipe, 24 pieces for the larger recipe. Roll each piece into a ball and flatten slightly. With thumb and forefinger, pinch the center of the circle until dough tears. Put finger through hole and stretch open. Place the circles on the baking sheets. Put in a warm place and let rise for 40 minutes.

When risen, pour 2 to 3 inches of oil into a wide saucepan and heat oil to 360°F, using a thermometer. Carefully remove several zeppoles from the baking sheet and drop into the hot oil. Zeppoles should not crowd each other. Cook for one minute, then turn each zeppole. Cook another minute or until both sides are golden brown. Remove, drain and place on paper towels. Make sure oil has remained at 360°F; lower or raise heat as needed. Add several more zeppoles and continue until all zeppoles are cooked.

Put some confectioner's sugar in a paper bag. Add zeppoles one or two at a time and shake to coat them with sugar. Knock off excess sugar.

These are best served warm. They can be kept in a warm oven while the others are cooking.

MORAVIAN SUGAR ROLLS

These sweet rolls with a sugary walnut topping come from the Moravians, a religious group that immigrated from Czechoslovakia and settled in Pennsylvania and North Carolina.

INGREDIENTS

MAKES 12	INGREDIENTS	MAKES 18
¼ cup	water	¼ cup
2 tbsp	powdered milk	3 tbsp
1	egg	2
½ cup	mashed potatoes	¾ cup
¼ cup	butter	6 tbsp
3 tbsp	honey	4½ tbsp
1 tsp	vanilla extract	1½ tsp
1 tsp	cinnamon	1½ tsp
½ tsp	salt	¾ tsp
2 cups	bread flour	3 cups
1½ tsp	yeast	2¼ tsp

TOPPING

MAKES 12	TOPPING	MAKES 18
2 tbsp	very soft butter	3 tbsp
¼ cup	brown sugar	6 tbsp
½ tsp	cinnamon	¾ tsp
pinch	ground nutmeg	¼ tsp
¼ cup	chopped walnuts	6 tbsp

METHOD

Put dough ingredients in bread pan in order suggested by your bread machine instructions. Set for white bread, dough stage. Press Start.

Butter muffin tins: 12 cups for the smaller recipe, 18 cups for the larger recipe. Make the topping by using a fork to mash together the butter, brown sugar and spices. Stir in the walnuts.

When dough is ready, turn out onto a lightly floured board and punch down. Roll into a rope. Cut smaller quantity into 12 equal pieces, larger into 18 pieces. Roll each piece into a ball – it does not have to be perfectly round – and put into a muffin cup. Turn so all sides are buttered. Spread some of the topping on each ball of dough.

Put in a warm place to rise for 1 hour. Bake in a preheated 350°F oven until dough is golden, 20 to 25 minutes.

NOTE

This recipe is based on pure mashed potatoes with no additions. If milk or other liquids have been added to the potatoes, check during kneading and add a little flour if dough is too wet.

BARM BRACK

Barm Brack is an Irish fruit bread, eaten on St Brigid's feast day, February 1. This is a heavy, sweet bread which tends to scorch when baked in the bread machine because of the high sugar content. It should be baked in the oven.

1lb LOAF	INGREDIENTS	1½lb LOAF
1	egg	2
½ cup	milk	⅔ cup
2 tbsp	butter	3 tbsp
3 tbsp	brown sugar	4½ tbsp
¼ tsp	cinnamon	½ tsp
¼ tsp	ground nutmeg	½ tsp
½ tsp	salt	¾ tsp
2 cups	bread flour	3 cups
2 tsp	yeast	1 tbsp
3 tbsp	candied orange peel	4½ tbsp
⅓ cup	golden raisins	½ cup

METHOD

Put all ingredients except orange peel and golden raisins in bread pan in order suggested by your bread machine instructions. Set for dough. Press Start. After about 15 minutes or when the beeper signals time to add fruit, add orange and raisins.

When dough is ready, punch it down on a lightly floured board. Let it rest a few minutes. Butter a 9½-inch loaf pan (can be smaller for smaller loaf). Shape the dough into a loaf and put it in the pan, turning so all sides are buttered. Cover and let rise in a warm place for 1 hour.

When bread has risen, bake in a preheated 350°F oven until the top is golden, about 30 to 45 minutes.

KOLACHE

Kolaches are individual Czechoslovakian pastries with fruit or cheese fillings, often eaten at Easter or Christmas. Below are recipes for two fillings, or you can use your favorite recipe for other fruit, nut, or poppyseed fillings. For special occasions, serve a variety of fillings.

MAKES 16	INGREDIENTS	MAKES 24
1	egg	1 + 1 yolk
½ cup	milk	¾ cup
50 g (2 oz)	butter	85 g (3 oz)
¼ cup	sugar	6 tbsp
½ tsp	salt	¾ tsp
2 cups	bread flour	3 cups
1½ tsp	yeast	2¼ tsp

confectioner's sugar

APRICOT FILLING
(Makes enough for 16 kolaches)

½ cup chopped dried apricots

⅓ cup sugar

2 tbsp apricot brandy, orange liqueur or orange juice

CHEESE FILLING
(Makes enough for 24 kolaches)

3 oz cream cheese, softened

⅔ cup ricotta cheese, watery liquids poured off

1 egg yolk

3 tbsp sugar

½ tsp fresh lemon juice

METHOD

Put all ingredients in bread pan in order suggested by your bread machine instructions. Set for white bread, dough stage. Press Start.

Lightly oil two baking sheets.

When dough is ready, remove from bread machine and punch down. Cut smaller recipe into 16 equal pieces, the larger recipe into 24 pieces. Roll each piece into a ball and flatten slightly. Place balls about 1 inch apart in baking pan. Cover loosely and set in a warm place to rise until doubled, about 45 minutes.

Preheat oven to 375°F. Gently use one finger to make an indentation in the top of each kolache, taking care not to deflate the roll. Gently widen the hole with your finger. Put about 1 tbsp of filling (see below) in each kolache. Bake until kolaches are golden brown, 15 to 20 minutes. Sprinkle with confectioner's sugar while still warm.

APRICOT FILLING

Put apricots in a small saucepan. Cover with water. Bring to a boil, then reduce heat to very low. Simmer until water evaporates, watching closely and stirring frequently so apricots do not scorch. Just as last bit of water evaporates, add sugar and liqueur and heat just until sugar dissolves, about 1 minute. Let cool slightly, then purée in blender or food processor.

CHEESE FILLING

Beat all ingredients together until smooth.

SOPAIPILLAS

These Mexican treats are coated with sugar and served with honey.

MAKES 16	INGREDIENTS	MAKES 25
⅓ cup	water	½ cup
⅓ cup	milk	½ cup
1 tbsp	lard or solid shortening	1½ tbsp
1 tbsp	sugar	1½ tbsp
½ tsp	salt	¾ tsp
2 cups	bread flour	3 cups
1½ tsp	yeast	2¼ tsp
	oil for frying	
	confectioner's sugar	

METHOD

Put all ingredients except oil and confectioner's sugar in bread pan in order suggested by your machine's instructions. Set for white bread, dough stage. Press Start.

When dough is ready, punch down. Let it rest about 5 minutes. Then, on a lightly floured surface, roll dough into a rectangle about ⅜ inch thick. Cut dough into 2-inch squares. Place squares on ungreased baking sheets. Cover loosely and put in a warm place to rise while you heat the oil, about 15 minutes.

Pour oil at least 3 inches deep into a deep skillet, wok, or saucepan. Heat oil to 350°F. Watch the oil temperature carefully, as it can climb quickly. Slide a few sopaipillas into the hot oil. Do not crowd them. Cook until golden, turning once. Total cooking time is 1½ to 2 minutes.

Remove sopaipillas from the oil, letting them drain for a few moments. Then put them on several layers of paper towels. Sprinkle with confectioner's sugar, or put sugar and sopaipillas in a paper bag and shake. Make sure the oil temperature returns to 350°F before you add the next batch.

PECAN CRESCENT ROLLS

With pecans, brown sugar, and cinnamon, these sweet rolls are irresistible.

MAKES 16	INGREDIENTS	MAKES 24
1	egg	1
⅔ cup	milk	1¼ cups
¼ cup	butter	6 tbsp
¼ cup	sugar	6 tbsp
½ tsp	salt	¾ tsp
2½ cups	bread flour	3¾ cups
2 tsp	yeast	1 tbsp
	FILLING	
2 tbsp	very soft butter	3 tbsp
⅓ cup	brown sugar	½ cup
1 tsp	cinnamon	1½ tsp
½ cup	finely chopped pecans	¾ cup

METHOD

Put all dough ingredients in bread pan in order suggested by your bread machine instructions. Set for white or sweet bread, dough stage. Press Start.

When dough is ready, remove it from the bread machine and punch it down. Cut the smaller recipe in two equal parts, the larger recipe into three parts. Let the dough rest for 5 minutes. Oil two or three baking sheets.

On a lightly floured surface, roll out each section of dough into a circle, about 8 inches in diameter. Spread surface with soft butter and sprinkle with mixed cinnamon and sugar, and pecans.

Cut each circle into eight wedges. Starting from the outside of the circle, loosely roll up each wedge toward the point. Stretch slightly and pull it into a curve. Set on the baking sheet with the point underneath.

Let the dough rise until doubled, about 1 hour. Bake in preheated oven 375°F, 12 to 15 minutes.

APPLE KUCHEN

Kuchen is an easy fruit-filled German coffee cake. This recipe is for an apple topping, but you can substitute soft fruits such as peaches or apricots and skip cooking the fruit before baking.

1 lb LOAF	INGREDIENTS	1½ lb LOAF
1	egg	1
½ cup	milk	⅞ cup
¼ cup	butter	6 tbsp
¼ cup	sugar	6 tbsp
½ tsp	salt	¾ tsp
2 cups	bread flour	3 cups
1½ tsp	yeast	2¼ tsp
	TOPPING	
3 cups	peeled and sliced apples	4½ cups
1 tsp	fresh lemon juice	1 tsp
¼ cup	bread flour or all-purpose flour	6 tbsp
¼ cup	sugar	½ cup
1 tsp	cinnamon	1½ tsp
2 tbsp	butter, softened	3 tbsp

METHOD

Put all dough ingredients in bread pan. Set for white or sweet bread, dough stage. Press Start.

Make the fruit topping while bread machine is working. Pre-cook the apples slightly to soften them. Put them in a saucepan with the lemon juice and about ¼ cup water. Bring water to a boil, then reduce heat and simmer apples, stirring frequently, until they are barely soft, 7 to 10 minutes. Add a little water if needed so apples don't scorch, but there should be as little liquid as possible in the pan when apples are done.

In the meantime, mix the flour, sugar, and cinnamon. When apples are done, toss them with about 3 tbsp of the topping. Mix the softened butter with the rest of the topping. Set apples and topping aside until dough is ready.

Butter a 10-inch round pan (I like to use a springform pan) or a 9-inch square baking pan for the smaller recipe, two 8-inch round pans for the larger one. When dough is ready, remove from pan and punch down. Let it rest 5 minutes. Roll dough out to fit baking pan or pans. Pat the dough into the bottom of the baking pan. Arrange apples on top of the dough. Sprinkle topping over apples. Cover kuchen and put it in a warm place to rise 15 to 20 minutes. Preheat oven to 350°F. (The short rising period will produce a denser, chewier dough. A longer rising period will produce a lighter, more bread-like dough.) Bake kuchen until edges of cake are golden brown, 30 to 35 minutes.

MOROCCAN BREAD

This is a heavy, coarsely textured bread, fragrant with anise. It is traditionally eaten with tagine, or Moroccan stew.

1 lb LOAF	INGREDIENTS	1½ lb LOAF
¾ cup	water	1¼ cups
¼ tsp	sugar	½ tsp
1½ tsp	anise seed	2¼ tsp
1 tsp	coarse salt	1½ tsp
½ cup	whole-wheat flour	¾ cup
1½ cups	bread flour	2¼ cups
2 tsp	yeast	1 tbsp

METHOD

Put all dough ingredients in bread machine pan. Set for whole-wheat bread, dough stage. Press Start.

When dough is ready, remove from pan and punch down. Shape it into a round loaf and place it on a baking sheet that has been sprinkled with cornmeal. Cover dough and put in a warm place to rise until doubled, 1 to 1½ hours.

Prick dough with a fork. Bake 12 minutes in a preheated 400°F oven, then reduce heat to 300°F and bake about 40 minutes longer, until top and bottom sound hollow when rapped with your knuckles.

BATH BUNS

Bath buns, named after the English city where they originated, are made of a sweet egg dough.

MAKES 8	INGREDIENTS	MAKES 12
1	egg	1 + 1 yolk
½ cup	milk	¾ cup
¼ cup	butter	6 tbsp
¼ cup	sugar	6 tbsp
¼ tsp	ground ginger	½ tsp
¼ tsp	mace	½ tsp
½ tsp	salt	¾ tsp
2 cups	bread flour	3 cups
2 tsp	yeast	1 tbsp
⅓ cup	currants (or raisins)	½ cup

GLAZE

1 egg
1 tbsp milk
1–2 tbsp sugar

METHOD

Put all dough ingredients except currants in bread pan in order suggested by your bread machine instructions. Set for white or sweet bread, dough stage. Press Start. Add the currants after the first kneading or when the machine signals it's time to add fruit.

Butter a baking sheet. When dough is ready, remove from bread machine and punch down. Cut smaller recipe into 8 pieces, the larger recipe into 12. Roll each piece into a ball. Place balls on baking sheet and slightly flatten each one. Cover loosely and set in a warm place to rise until doubled, about 45 minutes.

Preheat oven to 400°F. Make glaze by fork-beating egg and milk. Lightly brush tops of rolls with glaze and sprinkle with sugar. Bake until buns are golden brown, 15 to 20 minutes.

RIGHT Bath Buns

BROWN SUGAR PECAN BREAD

This is a slightly sweet bread. Try it toasted with cream cheese.

1 lb LOAF	INGREDIENTS	1½ lb LOAF
½ cup	water	¾ cup
¼ cup	milk	6 tbsp
2 tbsp	butter	3 tbsp
3 tbsp	brown sugar	4½ tbsp
1½ tsp	cinnamon	2¼ tsp
½ tsp	salt	¾ tsp
¼ cup	oat bran	6 tbsp
2 cups	bread flour	3 cups
1½ tsp	yeast	2¼ tsp
½ cup	chopped pecans	¾ cup

METHOD

Put all ingredients except pecans in bread pan in order suggested by your bread machine instructions. Set for white bread, medium crust. Press Start. Add pecans after first kneading or when machine beeps to add fruit or nuts.

SALLY LUNN BREAD

Sally Lunn bread originated in Great Britain, but the southern United States has claimed it as its own. Traditionally, it is baked in a tube pan.

1 lb LOAF	INGREDIENTS	1½ lb LOAF
⅓ cup	milk	½ cup
2	eggs	3
¼ cup	butter	6 tbsp
3 tbsp	sugar	4½ tbsp
½ tsp	salt	¾ tsp
2 cups	bread flour	3 cups
1½ tsp	yeast	2¼ tsp

METHOD

Put ingredients in bread pan in order suggested by your bread machine instructions. Set for sweet bread, light crust. Press Start.

Alternatively, to bake the bread in a tube pan in the oven, set bread machine for the dough stage. When ready, remove dough and punch it down. The larger loaf goes in a 9- or 10-inch tube pan. The small loaf will fit in a 6- or 7-inch tube pan or 5- or 6-cup soufflé or casserole dish. Butter the pan and turn the dough in it so all sides are buttered. Cover loosely, put in a warm spot to rise until doubled in volume. Bake in a preheated 350°F oven until golden and a skewer inserted in the bread comes out clean, 25 to 30 minutes.

LEFT Brown Sugar Pecan Bread

LAVOSH (ARMENIAN FLATBREAD)

Lavosh is a puffy flatbread that is crisper than pita bread, but softer than a cracker. Rounds of lavosh are broken into pieces, not cut. Eat lavosh plain or with butter.

MAKES 4	INGREDIENTS	MAKES 6
¾ cup	water	1¼ cups
3 tbsp	butter	4½ tbsp
1 tsp	salt	1½ tsp
2 cups	bread flour	3 cups
1½ tsp	yeast	2¼ tsp
1	egg	1
2 tbsp	water	3 tbsp
1–2 tsp	sesame or poppy seeds	2–3 tsp

METHOD

Put water, butter, salt, flour, and yeast in bread pan in order suggested by your bread machine instructions. Set for white bread, dough stage.

Remove dough and punch down. Cut into 4 pieces for smaller recipe, 6 pieces for larger recipe. Roll each piece between your hands to form a ball, then flatten each ball slightly. Let dough relax for 10 minutes or so. This will help the dough stretch when you roll it out. Otherwise, it will keep bouncing back to its original shape.

Preheat oven to 400°F. Make a wash by lightly beating egg with remaining water.

On a lightly floured surface, roll out the first round of dough until it is paper thin. Transfer to a greased baking sheet. Working quickly, brush it with the egg wash. Sprinkle with seeds. Put the first round in the oven immediately, and repeat the process with each round. Bake each lavosh until it is puffy and lightly browned, 8 to 12 minutes.

BEIGNETS

These small, diamond-shaped doughnuts are a staple in New Orleans, where they are traditionally eaten warm with café au lait.

MAKES 4 DOZEN	INGREDIENTS	MAKES 6 DOZEN
⅔ cup	milk	1¼ cups
1	egg	1
½ tsp	vanilla	¾ tsp
2 tbsp	butter	3 tbsp
¼ cup	sugar	6 tbsp
½ tsp	salt	¾ tsp
¼ tsp	nutmeg	½ tsp
2½ cups	bread flour	3¾ cups
1½ tsp	yeast	2¼ tsp

oil for frying

confectioner's sugar

METHOD

Put all ingredients except oil and confectioner's sugar in bread pan in order suggested by your bread machine instructions. Set for white bread, dough stage. Press Start.

When dough is ready, punch down. Let it rest about 5 minutes. Then, on a lightly floured surface, roll dough into a rectangle about ½ inch thick. Working at a diagonal to the edge of the rectangle, cut dough into 1½-inch strips. Then cut the strips into diamonds with a new series of cuts, almost but not quite perpendicular to the first. Place the diamonds on ungreased baking sheets. Cover loosely and put them in a warm place to rise for 45 minutes.

Pour oil at least 3 inches deep into a deep skillet, wok, or saucepan. Heat oil to 365°F. Watch the oil temperature carefully, as it can climb quickly. Slide a few beignets into the hot oil. Do not crowd them. They will bob back up to the surface. Cook until golden on the bottom, 2 to 3 minutes. Then turn and cook another 2 to 3 minutes on the other side. You may need to hold the beignets down with a large spoon or other cooking utensil to keep them from turning uncooked side up again.

When beignets are golden, remove them from the oil, letting them drain for a few moments over the oil. Then put them on several layers of paper towels. Sprinkle them with confectioner's sugar. Beignets should be served warm. You may put the cooked beignets in a warm oven while others are cooking. Make sure the oil temperature returns to 365°F before you add the next batch of beignets.

10

FESTIVAL BREADS

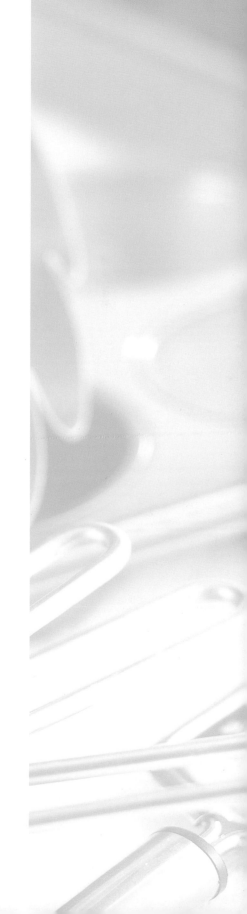

PANETTONE

This is an Italian Christmas bread distinguished by its tall, domed shape.

1 lb LOAF	INGREDIENTS	1½ lb LOAF
¼ cup	milk	6 tbsp
2	eggs	3
3 tbsp	butter	4½ tbsp
3 tbsp	sugar	4½ tbsp
½ tsp	salt	¾ tsp
1 tsp	grated lemon peel	1½ tsp
1 tsp	vanilla	1½ tsp
½ tsp	anise seed	¾ tsp
2 cups	bread flour	3 cups
2 tsp	yeast	1 tbsp
3 tbsp	pine nuts	4½ tbsp
2 tbsp	golden raisins	3 tbsp
¼ cup	chopped candied fruit	⅓ cup
1 tbsp	flour	1 tbsp

METHOD

Put all ingredients except pine nuts, raisins, fruit, and the last tablespoon of flour in bread pan in order suggested by your bread machine instructions. Set for white bread, dough stage. Press Start.

The high sugar content interferes with the rising action of the yeast, so it is kneaded after the first rising. Remove the dough and punch down. Toss candied fruit with 1 tbsp flour, then gently knead the fruit, raisins, and pine nuts into the dough. Put the dough in a buttered pan and turn so all sides are greased. Panettone is traditionally baked in a tall, cylindrical pan. Use a 1-pound coffee can or a 5-cup soufflé dish for the smaller loaf and a slightly oversized loaf pan or an 8-cup round casserole dish for the larger one. Set it in a warm place, cover loosely, and let rise until doubled in volume.

Bake in preheated 350°F oven until golden and skewer inserted comes out clean, 30 minutes.

LEFT Panettone

CHALLAH

Challah is an egg bread that is oven-baked for the Jewish Sabbath. It is usually a straight, braided loaf, but sometimes the braid is coiled like a snail. At Rosh Hashanah, it may be formed in a circle, symbolizing a prayer rising heavenward.

1 lb LOAF	INGREDIENTS	1½ lb LOAF
2	eggs	3
¼ cup	water	⅓ cup
1 tbsp	butter	1½ tbsp
2 tbsp	sugar	3 tbsp
1 tsp	salt	1½ tsp
2 cups	bread flour	3 cups
2 tsp	yeast	1 tbsp

GLAZE

1 egg yolk

1 tsp water

1–2 tsp poppy seeds

METHOD

Put ingredients in bread pan in order suggested by your bread machine instructions. Set for white bread, dough stage. Press Start.

When dough is ready, remove and punch down. Cut dough into three equal parts. Roll each piece into a rope about 12 inches long for the small loaf, 16 to 18 inches for the large loaf. Braid the three ropes together. Pinch the ends together and turn them under. Cover the loaf and set it in a warm place to rise until doubled in volume, 45 minutes to 1 hour.

Preheat the oven to 350°F. Make glaze by beating egg yolk and water with fork. Brush lightly over loaf. Sprinkle top with poppy seeds.

Bake until top is nicely browned, 30 to 35 minutes.

VANOCKA
(CZECHOSLOVAKIAN CHRISTMAS BREAD)

This is a braided loaf, seasoned with ginger and nutmeg and full of fruit and nuts. It takes some work to knead in the fruit and to make the elegant braids. The loaf is baked in the oven. This recipe will fit both the 1-pound and 1½-pound pans.

INGREDIENTS

⅔ cup milk

1 egg

¼ cup butter

¼ cup sugar

1 tsp salt

¼ tsp ground ginger

¼ tsp ground nutmeg

1 tsp grated lemon peel

3 cups bread flour

1 tbsp yeast

¼ cup slivered blanched almonds

¼ cup golden raisins

1 tbsp candied orange peel

1 egg yolk beaten with 1 tbsp water

2 tbsp sliced almonds

confectioner's sugar

METHOD

Put milk, egg, butter, sugar, salt, spices, lemon peel, flour, and yeast in bread pan in order suggested by your bread machine instructions. Set for white or sweet bread, dough stage. Press Start. You may add the almonds when the machine signals time to add fruit, but don't add the raisins and candied orange peel because the additional sugar in an already sweet bread could interfere with the yeast's rising action.

Oil a baking sheet at least 14 inches long. When the dough is ready, remove and punch down. Knead in the fruit and nuts. Cut the dough into four equal parts. Take three and roll each to form a rope about 18 inches long. Braid the ropes, pinch ends together, and place on the baking sheet.

Cut the remaining piece into four equal parts. Again, take three and roll each between your hands to form a thin rope about 18 inches long. Braid the ropes and center the braid on top of the fat braid. Run wetted fingers along the underside of the thin braid, then lightly press it onto the fat braid. Pinch the ends together and press them under the ends of the fat braid.

Cut the remaining piece into two equal parts. Roll each into a skinny rope about 16 inches long. Twist the two ropes together. Center the twist on the thin braid. Wet your fingers and run them lightly on the underside of the twist, then lightly press onto the thin braid. Pinch the ends together and turn them under. Use four or five toothpicks to skewer the braids in place. Otherwise, the top braids may slip off as the dough rises. Cover bread loosely, put in a warm place, and let rise until dough has almost doubled, about an hour.

Preheat the oven to 375°F. Lightly brush with the egg wash, then sprinkle the sliced almonds over the top and press a few into the sides. Bake until brown and a skewer inserted in a thick part comes out clean. Sprinkle with confectioner's sugar while warm.

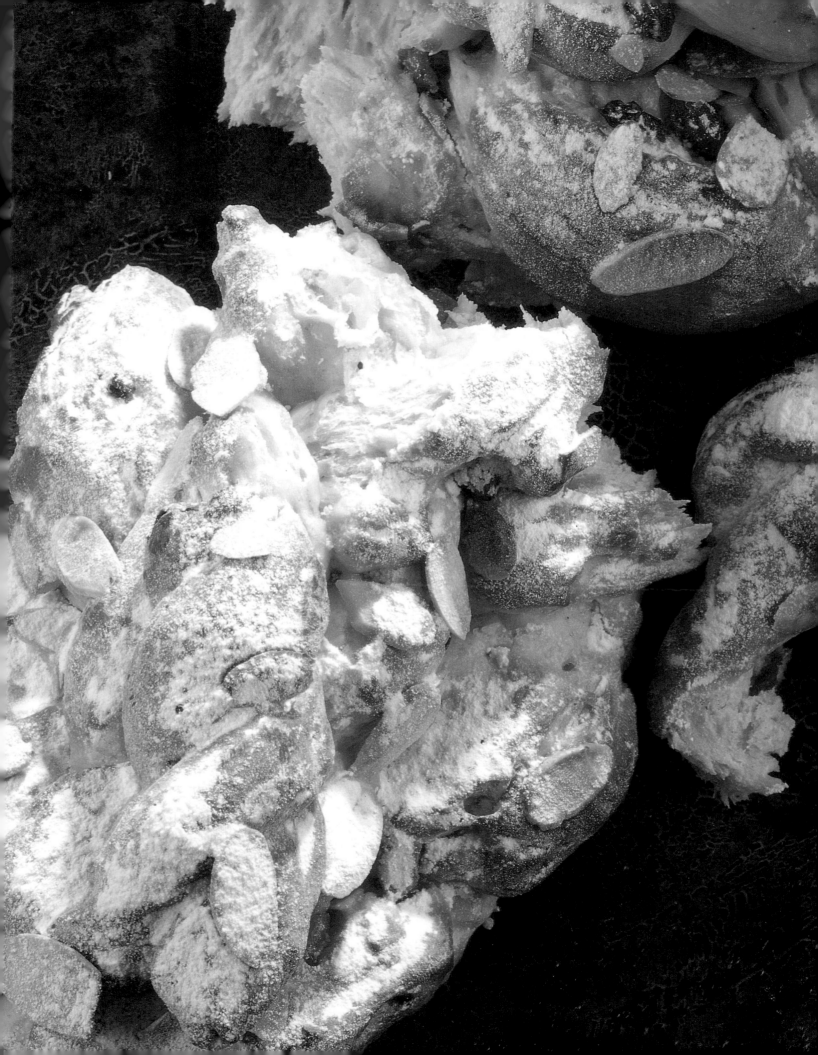

MORAVIAN SUGAR BREAD

Moravian Sugar Bread is a coffee cake that originated in Germany and was brought to the United States by Moravians who settled in North Carolina.

1 lb LOAF	INGREDIENTS	1½ lb LOAF
5 tbsp	milk	½ cup
1	egg	1 + 1 yolk
⅓ cup	mashed potatoes	½ cup
3 tbsp	butter	4½ tbsp
¼ cup	sugar	6 tbsp
½ tsp	salt	¾ tsp
2 cups	bread flour	3 cups
1½ tsp	yeast	2¼ tsp
	TOPPINGS	
¼ cup	brown sugar	⅓ cup
½ tsp	cinnamon	¾ tsp
¼ tsp	nutmeg	¼ tsp
3 tbsp	butter	4½ tbsp

METHOD

Put dough ingredients in bread pan in order suggested by your bread machine instructions. Use a 9-inch loaf pan for the smaller loaf and a 9-inch square baking pan for the larger one. Set for white or sweet bread, dough stage. Press Start.

When dough is ready, remove from bread machine and punch down. Put dough in a greased baking pan and turn so all sides of dough are greased. The mashed potatoes should be plain, with no butter, milk, or seasonings. Cover, put in a warm place, and let rise until doubled in bulk. Preheat oven to 375°F.

Make topping by combining all ingredients in a small saucepan. Heat, stirring often, until butter is melted and sugar is dissolved. With your fingertips, gently make shallow indentations all over the top of the dough. Spread topping across top of bread. Bake 30 minutes.

SWEDISH CHRISTMAS BREAD

This is a dark, dense rye bread made with stout or ale, flavored with orange peel and molasses, and studded with bits of candied orange peel. It is best eaten simply with butter.

1 lb LOAF	INGREDIENTS	1½ lb LOAF
¾ cup	dark stout or ale	1¼ cups
1 tbsp	vegetable oil	1½ tbsp
3 tbsp	molasses	4½ tbsp
½ tsp	salt	¾ tsp
¾ cup	bread flour	1 cup
1½ cups	rye flour	2¼ cups
1 tbsp	grated orange peel	1½ tbsp
2 tsp	yeast	1 tbsp
2 tbsp	candied orange peel	3 tbsp

METHOD

Put all ingredients except candied orange peel in bread pan in order suggested by your bread machine instructions. Set for whole-wheat bread, medium crust. Add candied orange peel after first kneading or when beeper indicates time to add fruit.

GREEK NEW YEAR'S BREAD

This bread, slightly sweet and flavored with orange, is traditionally eaten on New Year's Eve. The baker hides a coin in the bread, and the person who finds it will have good luck in the new year, according to Greek tradition.

1 lb LOAF	INGREDIENTS	1½ lb LOAF
1	egg	2 + 1 yolk
⅓ cup	milk	½ cup
¼ cup	butter	⅓ cup
¼ cup	sugar	6 tbsp
2 tsp	grated lemon peel	1 tbsp
2 tsp	grated orange peel	1 tbsp
½ tsp	salt	¾ tsp
2 cups	bread flour	3 cups
2 tsp	yeast	1 tbsp

GLAZE

1 egg white beaten with 2 tsp water
2–3 tbsp pine nuts
(you may substitute slivered almonds)
1–2 tbsp sugar

METHOD

Put all dough ingredients in bread machine pan. Set for white or sweet bread, dough stage. Press Start.

When dough is ready, remove from pan and punch down. Let it rest 5 minutes. Butter a baking sheet. Roll the bread into a rope, about 30 inches for smaller loaf, about 40 inches for larger loaf. Coil the rope into a circle on the buttered baking sheet. Insert a foil-wrapped coin into the dough from the underside, where it cannot be seen. Cover dough and put in a warm place to rise until doubled, 45 minutes to 1 hour.

Brush dough with egg-water wash. Stick pine nuts in the folds of the dough, following the circular pattern. Sprinkle with sugar.

Bake bread in preheated 375°F oven until golden, about 30 minutes.

ALSATIAN CHRISTMAS BREAD

This bread from the Alsace region of France is very different because it uses only enough brioche dough to hold a large quantity and variety of dried fruit together in a loaf. It is best when made with many different fruits – I use nine when I make it – but the selection can be varied. The fruit is marinated in Kirsch overnight. Although related to fruitcake, it uses a yeast dough and does not call for bitter ingredients such as candied citron that are traditional in fruitcake. The bread is traditionally served on Christmas Eve, or with breakfast on Christmas and New Year's Day. This is a sweet, dense bread that should be eaten in thin slices and does not need butter. Because the loaf uses such a small amount of bread dough, it does not matter what size machine pan you use.

FRUIT

A total of 4 cups of any combination
of the following chopped fruits:
dried apples, figs, golden raisins, dried
sweet cherries, dried apricots, dried peaches,
dates, dried pears, dried cranberries, dried
pineapple, dried mango
1 cup Kirsch or cherry-flavored brandy
¹⁄₂ tsp cinnamon
2 tbsp all-purpose or bread flour
1 cup chopped walnuts

BRIOCHE DOUGH

2 tbsp milk
1 egg
3 tbsp butter, at room temperature
1 tbsp sugar
¹⁄₄ tsp salt
1 cup bread flour
³⁄₄ tsp yeast

METHOD

The night before you make this bread, mix the fruits, Kirsch and cinnamon and let marinate.

The following day, put brioche ingredients in bread pan in order suggested by your bread machine instructions. Set for white bread, dough stage. Press Start.

While dough is working, drain the fruit well and discard the Kirsch. Mix the flour with the fruit, then stir in the walnuts. Lightly butter a loaf pan that is 8 to 9¹⁄₂-inches long.

When dough is ready, punch it down on a lightly floured board. Let it rest a few minutes. Put the dough in a large mixing bowl and mix in the fruit. As you do this, the dough will tear into bits. Shape the mixture into a loaf and place in buttered loaf pan.

Cover and put in a warm place for 45 minutes. You will not see a lot of rising. Place bread in a preheated 375°F oven and bake for 40 minutes.

APRICOT ALMOND BABKA

*Babka is a Polish holiday bread, related to brioche, rich with butter and eggs.
Because of the high amount of butter and liquids, it will not bake properly in the
bread machine and must be baked in the oven in a brioche pan, 10-inch Bundt pan,
or tube pan. This is a sweet babka, flavored with apricots and almonds. Because of
the type of pan that must be used, only a recipe for a 1½-pound loaf is given.*

INGREDIENTS

½ cup milk

3 eggs

8 tbsp butter at room temperature

⅓ cup sugar

1 tsp salt

1½ tsp vanilla extract

3 cups bread flour

2¼ tsp yeast

½ cup chopped dried apricots

¼ cup slivered almonds

3 tsp confectioner's sugar

METHOD

Put first eight ingredients in bread pan in order
suggested by your bread machine instructions. Set for
white bread, dough stage. Press Start. After about 15
minutes add apricots and almonds.

Butter the pan. If your bread machine has not punched
down the dough, gently work it between your hands
and squeeze out air. This is a very wet, sticky dough –
almost a batter – which cannot be kneaded in the usual
way; no flour should be added. Put the dough in the
baking pan and spread so it makes an even circle.

Cover with lightly buttered wax paper or plastic wrap.
Put in a warm place and let rise until doubled in size,
about 40 minutes.

Bake in a preheated 375°F oven, 30 to 35 minutes in a
Bundt or tube pan, 45 to 55 minutes in a brioche pan.
Test by sticking a knife in a deep spot in the bread. If it
comes out clean, bread is ready. Cool on a wire rack,
and sprinkle the sugar over the top.

CHERRY CHRISTMAS WREATH

This holiday bread is made with a sweet, buttery dough that is flavored with orange zest, vanilla, spices and dried cherries, then formed into a circle.

1LB LOAF	INGREDIENTS	1½lb LOAF
1	egg	1 + 1 yolk
7 tbsp	milk	⅔ cup
3 tbsp	butter	4½ tbsp
3 tbsp	sugar	4½ tbsp
½ tsp	salt	¾ tsp
1 tsp	grated orange zest	1½ tsp
½ tsp	ground ginger	¾ tsp
1 tsp	ground nutmeg	1½ tsp
1 tsp	vanilla extract	1½ tsp
2 cups	bread flour	3 cups
1½ tsp	yeast	2¼ tsp
⅓ cup	dried sweet cherries	½ cup
2 tbsp	sliced almonds	3 tbsp
1–2 tbsp	confectioner's sugar	2–3 tbsp

METHOD

Put all ingredients except cherries, almonds and confectioner's sugar in bread pan in order suggested by your bread machine instructions. Set for white bread, dough stage. Press Start. After about 15 minutes or when the beeper signals time to add fruit, add cherries.

When dough is ready, punch it down on a lightly floured board. Let it rest a few minutes, then take it between your hands and roll it into a rope, about 15 inches long for the smaller loaf, 18 to 20 inches for the larger. Put it on a nonstick or lightly buttered baking sheet. Bring the ends together to form a circle. Make diagonal cuts around the outside of the bread to resemble the points of leaves. Sprinkle almonds over dough and press lightly.

Cover and let rise for 45 to 60 minutes. Bake in a preheated 350°F oven until golden, about 30 to 40 minutes. Remove from oven and sprinkle with confectioner's sugar.

ITALIAN CHRISTMAS ROLL

Filled with fruit and nuts, this sweet loaf is from the Naples area, and is known in Italy as Rotolo di Natale. If you wish, you may adopt a modern tradition and mix one tablespoon of unsweetened cocoa with the fruit mixture. Brandy or rum can be substituted for the Marsala wine.

1lb LOAF	INGREDIENTS	1½ lb LOAF
	FILLING	
⅓ cup	chopped figs	½ cup
⅓ cup	chopped dried apples	½ cup
⅓ cup	golden raisins	½ cup
3 tbsp	sugar	4½ tbsp
3 tbsp	Marsala wine	4½ tbsp
1–2 tbsp	very soft butter	2–3 tbsp
⅓ cup	chopped walnuts	½ cup
¼ cup	pine nuts	6 tbsp
	BREAD	
1	egg	2
½ cup	milk	⅔ cup
3 tbsp	butter	4½ tbsp
¼ cup	sugar	6 tbsp
1 tsp	grated lemon zest	1½ tsp
1 tsp	almond extract	1½ tsp
1 tsp	salt	1½ tsp
2 cups	bread flour	3 cups
1½ tsp	yeast	2¼ tsp

TOPPING

1 egg, lightly beaten with 2 tsp water
1–2 tbsp sugar

METHOD

Preferably the night before baking, or at least several hours before, mix the fruits, sugar and Marsala wine for the filling. Stir well and let marinate.

The next day, put dough ingredients in bread pan in order suggested by your bread machine instructions. Set for dough stage. Press Start.

Drain any liquid off the fruit and discard.

When dough is ready, punch it down on a lightly floured board. Let it rest a few minutes, then roll it out into a rectangle about 10 x 15 inches for the smaller loaf, about 15 x 15 inches for the larger one. Spread the soft butter over the dough. Spread the drained fruit over the butter, then sprinkle walnuts and pine nuts over fruit.

Starting at a long end, roll the dough into a tight cylinder. Place the roll on a buttered baking sheet and pull ends together to form a circle. Cover, put in a warm place and let rise until doubled in bulk, about 1 hour.

Brush with egg wash and sprinkle with sugar. Bake in a preheated 375°F oven until brown, 25 to 40 minutes.

PAN DE MUERTOS (BREAD OF THE DEAD)

This sweet bread, flavored with orange peel and anise seed and decorated with skull and crossbones, is traditionally eaten in Mexico on the Day of the Dead. This is a day of celebration in Mexico, when relatives honor the dead by visiting their graves and leaving flowers and food there. This bread is shaped and baked in a conventional oven. The dough will fit in either the 1-pound or 1½-pound bread machine.

INGREDIENTS

¼ cup water	½ tsp anise seed
¼ cup milk	3 cups bread flour
2 eggs	1 tbsp yeast
¼ cup butter	1 egg white
¼ cup sugar	2 tbsp water
½ tsp salt	2 tsp sugar
1 tsp grated orange peel	¼ tsp cinnamon

METHOD

Put all but last four ingredients in bread pan in order suggested by your bread machine instructions. Set for white bread, dough stage. Press Start.

Grease a baking sheet. Make an egg wash by mixing the egg white and 2 tbsp water.

When dough is ready, remove it from the bread machine and punch down. Cut off about ⅓ cup of dough. Shape the rest of the dough into a large, round loaf about 2 inches high and place it on the baking sheet. Cut the small piece of dough into thirds. Roll two pieces between your palms to form skinny ropes. Flatten the ends a little so they look like bones. Dip them in the egg wash, then place them on top of the loaf in an X so they look like crossbones. Flatten the remaining piece of dough into a round, then pull it a little to elongate it so it looks like a skull. Dip it in the egg wash, then lightly press it onto the loaf, just above the crossbones. If desired, add tears or facial features.

Brush the loaf with egg wash. Cover the bread loosely. Set it in a warm place to rise until puffy, 30 to 45 minutes. Preheat oven to 375°F. Brush bread again with egg wash. Mix sugar and cinnamon and sprinkle over the bread. Bake until bread is browned and a little crusty, 30 to 35 minutes.

THREE KINGS BREAD

Three Kings Bread, or Rosca de los Reyes, is eaten in Mexico and Puerto Rico on Twelfth Night, January 6, the day the three kings brought Jesus gifts. A tiny ceramic doll, coin, or lima bean may be hidden in the bread. The person who finds it throws a party on Candle Mass, February 2.

1 lb LOAF	INGREDIENTS	1½ lb LOAF
1	egg	1 + 1 yolk
½ cup	water	¾ cup
2 tbsp	powdered milk	3 tbsp
¼ cup	butter	6 tbsp
3 tbsp	sugar	4½ tbsp
2 tsp	grated orange peel	1 tbsp
1 tsp	salt	1½ tsp
2 cups	bread flour	3 cups
2 tsp	yeast	1 tbsp
3 tbsp	chopped walnuts	4½ tbsp
2 tbsp	raisins	3 tbsp
3 tbsp	candied cherries	4½ tbsp

GLAZE

100 g (3½ oz) confectioner's sugar
1 tbsp milk or cream
¼ tsp vanilla

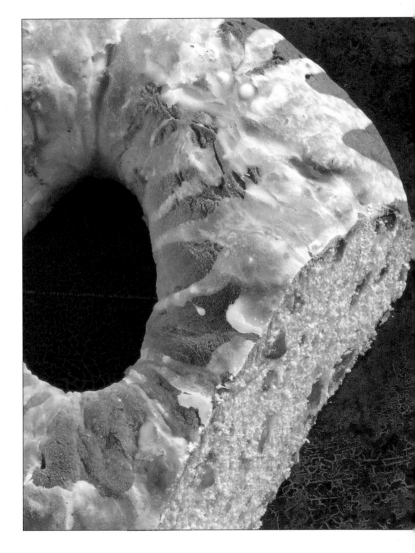

METHOD

Put all dough ingredients except fruit and nuts in bread pan in order suggested by your bread machine instructions. Set for white or sweet bread, dough stage. Press Start. Add fruit and nuts at beeper or after first kneading.

When dough is ready, remove from pan and punch down. Let it rest 5 minutes. Butter an 18-inch baking sheet. Roll the bread into a rope, about 24 inches for larger loaf. Bring ends of the rope together to form a ring, and place bread on baking sheet. Insert a ceramic doll, bean, or foil-wrapped coin into the dough from the underside. Cover dough and put in a warm place to rise until doubled, 45 minutes to 1 hour.

Bake bread in preheated 400°F oven until golden, about 25 minutes.

Make glaze by combining sugar, milk, and vanilla. The glaze should be thin enough to drizzle it, but not runny. Adjust milk if necessary. When bread has cooled slightly but is still warm, drizzle the glaze over the ring.

Hot Cross Buns

Hot Cross Buns, an English tradition, are eaten on Good Friday. Without the cross, they make delicious breakfast rolls year-round.

MAKES 12 to 16	INGREDIENTS	MAKES 18 TO 24
1	egg	1 + 1 yolk
½ cup	milk	¾ cup
¼ cup	butter	⅓ cup
¼ cup	sugar	6 tbsp
1 tsp	grated lemon peel	1½ tsp
½ tsp	cinnamon	¾ tsp
¼ tsp	nutmeg	½ tsp
⅛ tsp	ground cloves	¼ tsp
½ tsp	salt	¾ tsp
2 cups	bread flour	3 cups
2 tsp	yeast	1 tbsp
¼ cup	currants or raisins	½ cup

GLAZE

½ cup confectioner's sugar
1 tbsp milk or cream
½ tsp lemon juice

METHOD

Put all ingredients except currants or raisins in bread pan in order suggested by your bread machine instructions. Set for white bread, dough stage. Press Start. Add the currants or raisins after the first kneading or when the machine signals it's time to add fruit.

Lightly oil a 9-inch square pan or a 10-inch round pan for the smaller loaf, a 9 × 13-inch pan or two 8 × 8-inch square pans for the larger recipe.

When dough is ready, remove from bread machine and punch down. Cut smaller recipe into 12 to 16 equal pieces, the larger recipe into 18 to 24 pieces. Roll each piece into a ball. Place balls about ½-inch apart in baking pan. Cover loosely and set in a warm place to rise until doubled, 45 minutes to 1 hour.

Preheat oven to 375°F. With a sharp knife or razor blade, cut a cross in the top of each roll. Bake 12 to 15 minutes, until a skewer inserted in roll comes out clean.

Make glaze, adding sugar or milk if needed to give it a consistency that will allow you to drizzle it over the rolls but is not runny. Let rolls cool slightly but not completely. Drizzle icing in a cross, following the cuts in the top of the bun.

GREEK EASTER BREAD

This braided bread is made from a sweet egg dough flavored with lemon, vanilla and aniseed, but what sets it apart from other breads is the eggs, which are tucked whole into the braid and baked with the bread. If you wish, you may sprinkle 2 to 3 tablespoons of sesame seeds over the bread before baking.

1LB LOAF	INGREDIENTS	1½lb LOAF
1	egg	2
⅓ cup	milk	⅓ cup
1 tbsp	water	2 tbsp
⅓ cup	sugar	½ cup
¼ cup	butter	6 tbsp
1 tsp	grated lemon zest	1½ tsp
1 tsp	vanilla extract	1½ tsp
1 tsp	aniseed, preferably crushed	1½ tsp
1 tsp	salt	1½ tsp
2 cups	bread flour	3 cups
1½ tsp	yeast	2¼ tsp
¼ cup	golden raisins	6 tbsp
2–3	whole eggs, uncooked	4–5

EGG WASH

1 egg, beaten with a fork
2 tsp milk

METHOD

Put all dough ingredients except golden raisins and whole eggs in bread pan in order suggested by your bread machine instructions. Set for dough stage. Press Start. After about 15 minutes or when the beeper signals time to add fruit, add golden raisins.

When dough is ready, punch it down on a lightly floured board. Let it rest a few minutes. Then cut it into three equal pieces. Take each piece between your hands and roll it into a rope, about 12 to 14 inches long for the smaller loaf, 15 to 18 inches for the larger. Lay the three ropes on a nonstick or lightly buttered baking sheet. Beginning at one end, pinch the ends together and braid the three ropes, then pinch the bottom ends together. Bring the ends around to make a circle. Carefully ease the whole eggs between strands of dough.

Combine the egg and milk and brush it over the bread. Cover and let rise until bread has doubled in bulk, 45 to 60 minutes.

Place in a preheated 375°F oven and bake until the top is golden brown, about 30 to 35 minutes.

INDEX